FAMILY FORTUNES

Pressures on parents and children in the 1990s

Sue Middleton ✦ Karl Ashworth ✦ Robert Walker

CPAG Ltd, 1-5 Bath Street, London EC1V 9PY

CPAG promotes action for the relief, directly or indirectly, of poverty among children and families with children. We work to ensure that those on low incomes get their full entitlements to welfare benefits. In our campaigning and information work we seek to improve benefits and policies for low-income families, in order to eradicate the injustice of poverty. If you are not already supporting us, please consider making a donation, or ask for details of our membership schemes and publications.

Poverty Publication 89

Published by CPAG Ltd, 1–5 Bath Street, London EC1V 9PY
Tel: 0171 253 3406

ISBN 0 946744 68 8

The Joseph Rowntree Foundation has supported this project as part of its programme of research and innovative development projects, which it hopes will be of value to policy makers and practitioners. The facts presented and views expressed in this report, however, are those of the authors and not necessarily those of the Foundation.

The authors are grateful to the Department of Social Security (DSS) for permission to publish Chapter 10. The views expressed therein are those of the authors and do not necessarily reflect those of the DSS or any of its agencies.

The views expressed in this book are the authors' and do not necessarily express those of CPAG.

Cover and layout design by Devious Designs, 0742 755634
Cover photograph by Devious Designs
Typeset by Nancy White, 0171 607 4510
Printed by The Alden Press, 0865 249071

CONTENTS

ABOUT THE CONTRIBUTORS

Karl Ashworth is a Research Fellow in the Centre for Research in Social Policy (CRSP) at Loughborough University of Technology.

Karen Kellard is a Project Assistant in the CRSP at Loughborough University of Technology.

Sue Middleton is a Research Fellow in the CRSP at Loughborough University of Technology.

Anne Peaker is a Research Fellow in the CRSP at Loughborough University of Technology.

Michelle Thomas was a Student Researcher on placement at the CRSP at Loughborough University of Technology. She is currently at the University of Surrey, Guildford.

Robert Walker is Professor of Social Policy Research and Director of the CRSP at Loughborough University of Technology, and a member of CPAG's Policy Committee.

ACKNOWLEDGEMENTS

A book is always the product of far more people than simply those who claim authorship. This has been particularly so with *Family Fortunes*. We would like to thank the following colleagues and friends.

Carey Oppenheim who, as well as helping with the original research design, has advised throughout the project and also commented on the draft manuscript. The Joseph Rowntree Foundation, which funded this work and, in particular, Barbara Ballard, Senior Research Officer with the Foundation, who gave us unstinting support and encouragement throughout.

The members of our development committee, John Hills, Jane Millar, Louie Burghes, Alan Marsh and Diane Dixon, all helped, advised and suggested solutions to apparently intractable problems.

Bob Burgess, who acted as consultant for the work with children.

Jean Rushton and Rosie Porter, who performed miracles in recruiting and hostessing the group discussions.

The parent companies and managers of the individual stores in Leicester and Loughborough who gave permission for us to cost the budget standards described in Chapter One in their stores: Mothercare, Kwik Save, BhS, Superdrug, Comet Electrical Discount Warehouse and MFI.

Gerison Lansdown, Jonathan Bradshaw, Peter Golding and Sally Witcher who made valuable comments and suggestions on the draft manuscript. Thanks also to Vicky Fisher and Nancy White for production.

Our colleagues in the Centre for Research in Social Policy: Karen Kellard, Anne Peaker and Michelle Thomas who helped with the fieldwork; Rosie Woolley and Sharon Walker who coped with our unreasonable demands with their usual tolerance and fortitude; and Lisa Hull who helped with the final version of Chapter Three.

Above all, we wish to thank the mothers who took part in our group discussions and the children, parents and teachers who agreed to allow us into their classrooms. The enthusiasm which they brought to the project and their patience with our demands is unmatched in our experience of research.

And last but not least, our own fortunes: Jenny Middleton and Melissa and Oliver Walker, who not only helped us in the very early stages of the research, but have also had to suffer its consequences!

FOREWORD

We are all experts about children. After all, we have all been children in the recent or, perhaps, increasingly distant past. Many of us now have responsibility for children, with all the pain, bliss, anguish and joy which that can confer. On one thing, however, we can all pronounce with certainty: children cost.

The Child Poverty Action Group has always rooted its campaigns in the observation that the costs of child rearing are disproportionately borne by those who happen to have direct responsibility for their upbringing. These costs bear even more heavily on those parents on a low income. Our view has been that children, both as the next generation and as a peculiarly dependent group in the present generation, are the responsibility of the whole community. That shared burden is best met and represented by child benefit, still the most radical and comprehensive expression of the need to share the costs of children across the community.

In recent work CPAG has charted the true costs of children.[1] Using a well-formulated budget standard, the study found that 'income support – the safety net which provides the minimum amount of income for people to live on ... meets only 78 per cent of the low cost budget of a child in a two adult, two child family...' And that low-cost budget, it must be noted, was itself 26 per cent less than the 'modest-but-adequate' standard employed in the research.

But the costs of a child are socially determined, and to discover what they are means listening to parents and children. The research reported in this book is the most detailed recent study of the financial pressures facing parents in the 1990s. The authors show how children soon learn not only what is expected of them by their peers, but, for many, how limited their parents' means are to meet those expectations. Not surprisingly, with financial strictures come emotional costs. The journey from trainer culture to tantrum culture is a short one.

The lesson is not that children demand ever more. Nor that in a culture devoted to conspicuous consumption, indulgent wants have outstripped sensible needs, as those only too quick to condemn a child's sense of exclusion as the triumph of greed over necessity will sometimes smugly assert. We live in a society in which some have the privilege not only to consume, but to define the consumption patterns and aspirations of others. In Townsend's seminal formulation: 'Individuals, families and groups in the population can be said to be in poverty when they lack the resources to obtain the types of diet, participate in the activities and have the living conditions and amenities which are customary, or are at least widely encouraged and approved, in the societies to which they belong.'[2] There is no society so demanding as that of childhood.

A child may well survive being left out of the school trip to the coast, not being able to buy and bring home the cake s/he so lovingly baked at school, having cheap though functional trainers unadorned by designer logos, having no access to the varied joystick gratifications of Wing Commander or Lemmings. But surviving these deprivations is not enough. We are entitled to expect all children to be able to share the culture, pastimes, pleasures and experiences which society can offer them. This certainly cannot be so in a society in which 4.1 million children, 32 per cent of the total, live in poverty; in which the poorest 10 per cent of families with children had an average household income £438 per annum lower in real terms in 1992 than in 1979, a period in which the disposable annual income of the richest 10 per cent rose by £13,900.

This careful and innovative study meticulously charts the pressures created by the widening gulf between the demands and expectations imposed on poorer parents and children and their financial capacity to meet them. The authors demonstrate how even the most rudimentary calculus of what is required adequately to provide for children substantially exceeds what is provided by the social security system. And that calculus is not the result of 'expert' judgement nor of statistical pedantry. It derives from the considered and circumspect judgement of those who know best – the parents themselves.

The lessons are clear. The gap between the large minority of poor families in Britain and those more comfortably provided for is growing. That gap is corroding the family life of millions, excluding nearly one-third of all children from much of the routine comforts, pleasures and necessities which others take for granted. The cost of meeting their needs is the creation of an adequately progressive tax system, decent and fairly administered social security benefits, a child benefit restored to its real value and purpose, employment opportunities for the many denied access to the labour market, and proper incomes for those in it whose resources are suppressed by inadequate wage protection and poverty pay.

The real cost of not meeting these needs is in the truncated lives of children denied full access to the society in which they live. Their fortune is our responsibility.

Peter Golding

NOTES

1. N Oldfield and A C S Yu, *The Cost of a Child: living standards for the 1990s*, CPAG, 1993, p60.
2. P Townsend, *Poverty in the United Kingdom*, Penguin Books, 1979, p31.

Introduction
Sue Middleton and Robert Walker

DEFINING CHILDHOOD POVERTY IN BRITAIN

This book is about the economic pressures on children and parents in Britain and how they cope with these demands. The unifying theme is the pressure for children to be able to participate fully in the life of the community in which they live, to fit in with their peers, to have the same access to opportunities as those children with whom they live, play and go to school. The negative corollary of participation, namely exclusion (being singled out, being different), is shown to represent the worst fears of parents and children alike. Yet does such exclusion mean that a child can be said to be 'poor'?

The main protagonists in recent debates about childhood poverty in Britain are represented by two seemingly contradictory schools of thought: that childhood poverty no longer exists in Britain; and that childhood poverty not only exists but is affecting increasing numbers of children. Supporters of the 'end of childhood poverty' thesis point to the disappearance of barefooted children from our streets, the fact that British children no longer starve to death and ever increasing levels of affluence among all sections of the population. Proponents of the 'increasing levels of childhood poverty' school of thought draw attention to the large and increasing numbers of British children who live in families with the lowest incomes in society,[1] and to the increasing gap between the richest and the poorest families in Britain.[2]

The difference between these two schools of thought lies in their definitions of 'poverty'. For those who believe that poor children no longer exist, poverty is equated with the life and death experiences of children living in developing countries. For those who argue that childhood poverty not only continues to exist but affects ever larger numbers of children, poverty is a more relative concept. Although not usually life-threatening, such poverty is said nevertheless to result in real and lasting damage to those children who experience it. For example, the least affluent children in society continue to experience lower birthweights, worse health and lower levels of educational achievement than their wealthier peers.[3]

Debates about the definition of childhood poverty have largely ignored the fact that a definition is now enshrined in British law. Britain is a signatory to the 1991 United Nations Convention on the Rights of the Child, ratified by the British Government in 1991. Article 27 of the Convention asserts

> the right of every child to a standard of living adequate for the child's physical, mental, spiritual, moral and social development.

This and other articles of the Convention make clear that childhood poverty should no longer be defined solely by the lack of sufficient resources to maintain life but

> must take into account the needs of the child relative to standards which are considered to be acceptable within that society.[4]

Article 27.1, for example, stresses that children should have opportunities to participate in social activities accepted as a part of childhood. Article 30 asserts the right to an environment in which safe play and recreational opportunities exist.

Ratification of the Convention should have seen an end to arguments that, because children are not starving in Britain, childhood poverty does not exist. The Convention makes it clear that, in order not to be 'poor', a child has to experience a standard of living which allows her/him to participate *fully in the society in which s/he is growing up*. Conversely, childhood poverty implies exclusion from mainstream society and denial of the same access to opportunities that exists for the majority of children.

The Convention leaves unanswered a number of questions: what do children need to ensure that they are not excluded from mainstream society; how are those needs to be measured and costed; where do the pressures for children to have and do certain things come from; and how do parents and children cope with such pressures?

LISTENING TO PARENTS AND CHILDREN

This book attempts to answer some of these questions from the point of view of parents and children themselves. It is based on the findings of two innovative pieces of research undertaken by the Centre for Research in Social Policy (CRSP) between September 1993 and April 1994.[5] Most of the evidence comes from research funded by the Joseph Rowntree Foundation (JRF), which was carried out in association with the Child Poverty Action Group (CPAG). The main aim of this research, which involved talking to separate groups of parents and children, was to prepare for the first-ever national survey of family expenditures on children, which is to commence in early 1995 and is also to be funded by the JRF.

The second piece of research, which forms the basis of Chapter Ten, 'How mothers use child benefit', was partly funded by the Department of Social Security (DSS) to update knowledge about mothers' uses of, and attitudes to, child benefit. The role of child benefit was discussed by the first six groups of parents who took part in the JRF research, and the DSS funded two additional groups to focus on the topic.

Around 200 mothers and 130 children from different parts of the country and a range of socio-economic backgrounds took part in the development work. The exclusion of fathers from the research was not deliberate, except for the two groups dedicated to child benefit. We recruited parents who 'had the major responsibility for day-to-day expenditures on children'. In the event, all these turned out to be mothers.

The participation of the children was particularly important to us, given the emphasis in the UN Convention on the right of children to be consulted.[6] It is disappointing that the voices of children are heard rarely in social policy research, for children are arguably best placed to describe their own experiences and preoccupations. In any event, both they and the parents who took part had a great deal to say about the experience of being a parent and of being a child in Britain in the 1990s.

The book contains some statistical evidence, particularly in the first three chapters, but, in the main, consists of the results of qualitative analysis of the discussions which took place. Such analysis does not allow, and is not intended to make, statements and predictions about the behaviour of parents and children in the population as a whole. However, it does provide insights into the priorities, attitudes and concerns of the mothers and children who took part in the research to a depth, and with a degree of richness, which would be difficult using purely statistical evidence. Extensive use is made of verbatim quotations from the discussions with both children and mothers. These are included for illustrative purposes and should be read in the context of the surrounding text.

Wherever possible, we have allowed the parents and children to speak for themselves, although names have been changed in quotations in order to protect their anonymity. The number in brackets following the name of each mother refers to the socio-economic group to which she belongs. Following each quotation, the age of the children being discussed by that group of mothers is appended. Quotations from the children are followed by an indication of the socio-economic group, sex and age of each child.

The key below describes the conventions and abbreviations for quotations.

Socio-economic group of parents	Socio-economic group of children	Sex of children	Age of children
(1) = professional or managerial	MA – more affluent	M – male	8 years
(2) = other non-manual and skilled manual workers	LA – less affluent	F – female	11 years
(3) = semi- and unskilled workers and IS recipients		GU – gender unknown[7]	13 years
			16 years

To the best of our knowledge, this is the first time that research has systematically addressed the economic circumstances of children and the economic negotiations between parents and children from their own perspectives. The enthusiasm which both mothers and children brought to the task was unparalleled in our experience. It provides further evidence of the importance of actually listening to the views of parents and children whom researchers, journalists, politicians and pundits often enjoy criticising but all too rarely consult. As this research clearly shows, being a parent and, indeed, being a child, is not easy in 1990s Britain.

CHILDHOOD POVERTY AND EXCLUSION IN BRITAIN

Any attempt to assess the extent of childhood poverty as defined by the UN Convention on the Rights of a Child must begin by identifying what children need in order to ensure that they are not excluded from mainstream society. In other words, what standard of living is 'adequate' for a child growing up in Britain in 1994. The first section of the book presents the answers that parents and children gave to this question.

Chapter One describes a unique exercise in which parents from different parts of the country and from all socio-economic backgrounds were asked to draw up and agree minimum essential budgets for children of different ages. Conventional budget standards methodology, while invaluable in some respects, relies in the last analysis on the judgements of experts and researchers. Their decisions may bear little resemblance to the priorities and expenditure choices of parents themselves. The minimum budgets described in Chapter One represent the consensus reached by parents as to the absolute minimum standard of living which every child needs in order to ensure that s/he does not experience the poverty of exclusion.

Comparison of these budgets with income support (IS) levels suggest that many children in Britain are growing up in families which cannot afford to spend the minimum recommended by parents. For example, the IS level for a dependent child aged from six to ten years (including family premium) would need to be increased by £7.44 per week to achieve the minimum standard of living agreed by parents.

In Chapters Two and Three children tell us about what they own, how they spend their time and what they feel they need in order to participate in the world around them. It is clear that children have similar pressures and the same aspirations whatever their socio-economic background. This common culture of acquisition provides an indication of the economic pressures on poorer families. From our research it is clear that low-income families are making sacrifices in other areas of their limited budget in order to provide for their children. While poorer children experience similar pressures, the evidence in Chapter Two suggests that less affluent children have far fewer opportunities to benefit from time spent with their parents away from home, even on day trips. It is also apparent that they learn to limit their aspirations in this regard from a very early age.

Three of the major sources of pressure on children are examined in Chapters Four, Five and Six. Chapter Four describes the pressure that children experience to conform to the clothing norms of their peers and highlights the exclusion and abuse which sometimes result for children who cannot afford to wear the 'right' clothes. Chapter Five is devoted to expenditures related to school. Parents describe the financial pressures which the education system imposes on them and their fear of the social and educational exclusion that children suffer when parents cannot afford to meet these financial demands. Chapter Six explores children's awareness of, and attitudes to, advertising and its impact on them. Advertising inevitably helps to forge the common culture of acquisition and to fix the parameters of social exclusion in childhood.

The pressures which children experience from friends, school and advertising become financial demands on their parents and other family members. Chapters Seven and Eight describe the strategies and tactics which children use to persuade adults to buy them the things they want and those, in turn, which parents employ to resist or negotiate such demands. Of crucial importance, these chapters begin to document the different experiences and opportunities open to children and parents from varying socio-economic backgrounds and to reveal the nature of relative deprivation in Britain today. Chapter Seven suggests that, while all children argue, persuade, plead and threaten, children from less affluent families may be more likely to resort to those strategies which they know to be least effective – banging doors, shouting and so on.

The explanation for this may lie in the evidence in Chapter Eight that poorer parents not only have to say 'no' to their children more often, but are less able to respond consistently than richer parents. Week-to-week fluctuations in the financial demands on a tight budget mean that a child's request acceded to today may be turned down next week. The child may not always appreciate the reasons for this apparent inconsistency, a situation which must add further to the frustration at being denied that which s/he desperately desires.

Chapter Eight shows that poorer children miss out on another valuable lesson. Mothers believe that it is through negotiating financial deals and transactions with parents that children learn budgeting skills and strategies. Less well-off families often cannot afford the risk that money might be wasted in the process of their children learning the financial facts of life.

However, saying 'no', or giving in gracefully, are only two ways in which parents cope with the financial demands of children. Chapters Nine and Ten describe the lengths to which parents go in order to assure their children's participation in society and to protect them from exclusion. Chapter Nine explores some of the strategies which all parents, but particularly poorer ones, bring to household financial management. They maximise the total sum of resources available and, contrary to conventional wisdom, other family members and friends continue to play a crucial role in this. Mothers then perform financial miracles to ensure that resources are stretched as far as possible. Many parents make sacrifices in the interests of their children. Richer parents may go without clothes and entertainment in order to ensure that their children can have access to the things they 'want' (for example, holidays with the school). Poorer parents need to make more frequent and serious sacrifices just to provide the basics. Often they go without food so that their children can eat.

Chapter Ten illustrates the use of child benefit as a financial tool within the sophisticated budgetary strategies employed by mothers. It is clear that child benefit, used in a variety of ways, continues to make an important contribution to the family budget for all mothers. It is valued particularly as a regular, identifiable, lump sum which is paid to them on behalf of their children.

The final chapter concludes that the reality of poverty for children in Britain can most usefully be understood in terms of their exclusion from the 'physical, mental, spiritual, moral and social' world of their peers. However skilled, determined and self-sacrificing their parents, many children are being denied access to the material possessions and opportunities open to their friends, allowing them to be singled out by reason of their poverty. This is not the poverty of envy but of exclusion. Children are being denied not only what others consider commonplace, but what parents agree is essential for the well-being of all children.

Does this matter? Is it saying anything more than that some children come from richer families than others? Can Britain afford to ensure that the 'right of every child to a standard of living adequate for the child's physical, mental, spiritual, moral and social development' is met? The mothers to whom we listened were emphatic that the social consequences of not guaranteeing an adequate standard of living for all children were unthinkable. They were clear that society in general, and governments in particular, can, and must, make children the overriding priority in the allocation of resources. To quote one mother:

Adrienne (2) 'I think people should look at all children as assets for the future, whoever they belong to, and to make sure that they are looked after, provided for. They are our future aren't they? When we're pensioners, they'll be paying for us.'
            6 – 16 years

NOTES

1. The most recent figures suggest that in 1991/92 4.1 million children in Britain, 32 per cent, were living in 'poverty' (defined as half of average income after housing costs), with a further 9 per cent living on the 'margins of poverty' (defined as between 50 and 60 per cent of average income after housing costs). Department of Social Security, *Households Below Average Income: a statistical analysis 1979 – 1991/92*, HMSO, 1994.

2. See, for example, S Jenkins, *Winners and Losers: a portrait of the UK income distribution during the 1980s*, University of Wales, Swansea: Department of Economics Discussion Paper No. 94-07, 1994. This shows that the share of total income received by the poorest 10 per cent of the population has decreased from 4.3 per cent in 1979 to 2.9 per cent in 1990/91. Conversely, the richest 10 per cent of the population has increased its share of total income from 20.9 per cent to 27.4 per cent over the same period.

3. Central Statistical Office, *Social Focus on Children*, HMSO, 1994.

4. Children's Rights Development Unit, *UK Agenda Report 4: an adequate standard of living*, Children's Rights Development Unit, 1994.

5. A more detailed description of the methods used can be found in the Appendix.

6. Article 12, United Nations Convention on the Rights of the Child.

7. In some cases it proved impossible to identify from a small number of the taped group discussions whether the child speaking was a boy or a girl.

The 'bare essentials': parents' minimum budget for children

Sue Middleton and Michelle Thomas

COSTING A CHILD

What does it cost to bring up a child in Britain today? A simple answer would be to say that any child costs as much as her/his parents can afford and are prepared to spend. This answer is acceptable as long as all children live in families which have sufficient financial resources to meet their 'basic needs'. However, it is generally recognised that at any one time a proportion of children in Britain will be living in families whose income is insufficient to meet such 'basic needs'. In these circumstances, it is accepted that society has a responsibility to provide sufficient resources through the benefits system to ensure that children and their families at least can survive.

The problem is that no widely accepted definition exists of what constitutes the 'basic needs' of a child and what level of expenditure is required to meet those needs. Unlike many other countries, Britain does not have an official 'poverty line' – an agreed level of income or expenditure below which people are considered to be living in poverty. Levels of income support (IS), the benefit most often paid to families with no other source of income, are often used as a substitute for such a poverty line. However, although the basis on which IS levels are calculated is unclear, it apparently owes much to the original definitions of basic needs drawn up by Seebohm Rowntree in the early years of this century.

Budget standards are one method by which the basic needs of families can be defined and costed. Groups of experts come together to consider different budget areas and compile a basket of goods and services which they consider to be necessary for a particular family type to maintain a pre-determined standard of living. The Family Budget Unit at the University of York has used this methodology recently to produce a series of costed budgets for families of different types, among which is a low-cost budget for children of different ages.[1] This was published by CPAG in 1993 as *The Cost of a Child*, by Nina Oldfield and Autumn S Yu.[2]

One problem with using budget standards in defining basic needs is that the decision whether or not to include items from the baskets of goods and services rests ultimately with the particular group of experts and researchers who make up the budget standards committees. Their decisions do not necessarily relate to the priorities and actual expenditures of real families or real children. For example, parents might have a very different view of what constitutes children's basic food needs from that of the nutritional expert who is concerned solely with the provision of a 'healthy' diet. Yet it is parents who are meeting the day-to-day demands of children and who, presumably, are best placed to answer the question, what does a child cost?

AGREEING THE BUDGET STANDARD

The groups of parents in this study were asked to act as their own 'budget standards committees'.[3] Parents from different socio-economic groups, living in different parts of the country, and having at least one child in each of four age groups, were recruited.[4] Prior to attending the group, they were asked to complete a number of inventories, diaries and questionnaires in pre-determined budget areas which related to the particular child for which they had been recruited. When the groups met, parents were asked to allocate each of the items in their inventories and diaries to one of three categories; 'Essential', 'Desirable' or 'Luxury'. They were not given a definition of these categories but were asked to consider 'minimum essential' in the light of Article 27 of the United Nations Convention on the Rights of the Child, to which Britain is a signatory, namely:

> the right of every child to a standard of living adequate for the child's physical, mental, spiritual, moral and social development.

They were then told that we wished them to produce an agreed list of items and activities which they felt to be an essential minimum for a child in the relevant age group living in Britain today. They worked through the lists, deciding among themselves which items were essential. These were written up on a flip chart and, once each list was complete, they were asked to consider whether they had been too generous or too restrictive. Parents also considered numbers, quality, expected life, source of items and, more generally, the meaning of 'minimum essential'. The resulting lists were then presented to other groups of parents in order to ensure that the final baskets of goods and services represented a consensus among parents.

It is worth emphasising that our budget standard has been costed on the basis of decisions made by parents. The researchers intervened as little as possible in the discussions and negotiations which took place between parents in reaching a consensus. Once the final lists were agreed, these were costed by researchers at shops recommended by parents. Where no named store had been recommended, 'middle of the range' stores were used, since this was the range recommended by mothers, taking into account quality and price. Each store was contacted prior to our visit and we are grateful for the co-operation of the store managers. Costings were carried out in March 1994.

MINIMUM ESSENTIAL BUDGETS

Table 1 shows the minimum essential budget standard which parents drew up for both boys and girls in four age groups. Most of the difference in cost between boys and girls is accounted for by clothing and arises from a combination of the mothers insisting that girls require different clothing from boys, and the budget costing for boys' shoes, which were more expensive than for girls in the two- to five-year age group. It is assumed throughout that the child lives in a family of four, two adults and two children, in order to apportion the cost of those budget items, such as a washing machine, which parents decided should be allocated equally to each family member.

In drawing up their lists, the emphasis which mothers gave to the right of every child to participate fully in the life of the community was striking. They reiterated the need for every child to be able to 'fit in', not to be 'singled out' from their peers.

Naomi (3)   'With your first, it's got to have everything in't it? If it'd got to have a bright red nose you'd punch it.'
             Under 2 years

Rose (2)   'That's what it's all about, it's fitting in.'
Emma (1)   'Oh yeah, fitting in.'

Chris (2)	'To be the same as everyone, or to have the same chances as everybody else.'
Leslie (3)	'...which one of us would stand up and make our child stand out...?'
Chris (2)	'That's right, you wouldn't.'
Diane (2)	'Oh no, you'd never want your child to be the one who comes home crying at the end of the day.'

11 – 16 years

TABLE 1: **Parents' minimum essential budget standard (£ per week)**

	Under 2 years	2-5 years	6-10 years	11-16 years
Food	6.85	9.36	9.72	10.11
Clothes: girl	5.57	7.13	6.94	5.83
boy	5.41	8.65	6.49	6.34
Possessions and equipment	4.75*	3.13*	2.20	4.13
Activities	1.75	7.53	7.45	7.36
Furniture and decorating	0.17	0.54	0.54	0.54
Laundry	0.86	0.86	0.62	0.62
Toiletries: girl	6.54**	2.18**	0.65	2.45
boy	6.54	2.18	0.65	1.99
Total girl	**26.49**	**30.73**	**28.12**	**31.04**
boy	**26.33**	**32.25**	**27.67**	**31.09**

* includes baby equipment such as pushchair, car seat
** includes disposable nappies

The mothers emphasised the importance for all children to have access to a range of activities and opportunities in order to develop properly. They felt that the consequences for society of children being excluded from such participation were serious.

Sandra (2)	'If they see other children doing it and you don't give them any, they're going to feel left out and they'll resent you for it. When they're old enough they're going to go out and do all the naughty things that you don't want them to do.'

6 – 10 years

Jan (1)	'I mean, it sounds exaggerated, but you don't know, if you

tell them they can't do anything because you can't afford it, are they going to turn to other means to get the money so they can do it? ... I mean you don't know what road you're pushing them down, you know, crime and ...'

6 – 10 years

This is not to say that parents were unaware of the dangers of giving children too much or of giving in to the combined pressures of television and their peers, as will be clear from later chapters of this book. Their budgets did not make allowance for designer label clothes, videos or even computers, despite a recognition of the increasing educational pressure for children to have access to computers at home. In fact, parents felt that their lists represented an absolute basic minimum, and would have been devastated if this was all their own children had.

Ann (2) 'I mean you've not given them the things you'd like to give them, you're only giving them the bare essentials.'

Sandy (2) 'How would you feel if your children had to manage on that?'

Laura (3) 'Gutted.'

6 – 10 years

FOOD

The budget standards for food assume that the child takes a packed lunch to school. It makes no allowance for the provision of free school meals which, as some mothers pointed out, are not available during school holidays. Interestingly, some mothers whose children were eligible for free school meals stated that they did not take this up, preferring to provide a packed lunch to ensure that the child was eating properly and to avoid any possibility of the child being 'singled out'.

June (3) 'I'm a bit ashamed to say it but I don't want other people to know that my child gets free school dinners. When I was at school about 18 years ago you were looked down upon.'

Terry (3) 'I had that and I felt ashamed.'

0 – 5 years

Liz (3) 'You see I could actually get free school dinners, but he takes a pack up because he wouldn't eat them.'

6 – 10 years

The food budget has been costed on the basis of a consensus diet for each age group. The consensus included agreement on the quantities, quality and variety necessary. Mothers made an allowance for 50 pence per week for sweets in each of the age groups, which they justified on the grounds that failure to do so would exclude a child from full participation with their peers.

Kelly (3)   'I wouldn't like to think that my children never got any sweets because I couldn't afford to buy them. I think it's essential in that way. You imagine, this poor child going out to play and his friends having sweets, and he'd be saying "I've never had one before". You should be able to afford to go down the shops once a week and buy him a packet of sweets.'

Under 2 years

The food budget for the under-two-year age group assumes that the child is bottle-fed, and allows for a 'weaning' diet.

While mothers were aware of the need for, and content of, a healthy diet, they were more concerned with the need to avoid waste. For example, in discussing whether the budget should allow for cheaper white bread, or more expensive but healthier wholemeal bread, mothers decided on a mixture of the two, emphasising that there is little point buying wholemeal bread if children refuse to eat it.

CLOTHES

The budget for clothes for the 6-10- and 11-16-year age groups assumes that the child attends a school where basic school uniform is required. Mothers agreed that any school uniform required by the school is an essential minimum for the child, again to ensure that the child is not singled out.

Jackie (2)   'If the majority are wearing it and they're going to feel left out, then yes, it is essential.'

Karen (3)   'What I'm saying is if they're going to be made a scapegoat for not wearing it, they've got the right to have it.'

6 – 10 years

Mothers then specified a minimum essential quantity of items of school clothing. Budgets have been costed according to the replacement cycle also specified by the mothers. For example, for the child aged six to ten, mothers agreed that all clothing, except shoes, pants, socks and tights, would need to be replaced once a year. A minimum of three pairs of new, properly fitted shoes per year were allowed, whereas two replacements per year of pants, socks and tights were felt to be essential.

POSSESSIONS

Children's possessions were defined as all those things that a child owns or to which s/he has access other than clothing and bedroom furniture and fittings. The budget for possessions covers such items as toys, games, books, stationery. Mothers felt that it was vital to the development of the child to have at least some possessions.

Stephanie (2) 'I mean you could say, "Right, they don't need toys, they don't need anything", but they need some stimulation, or else what are they going to be like when they're older...?'
2 – 5 years

Mothers also reached a consensus that access to a colour television for the family is an essential minimum for a child in Britain today, although a video recorder is not and was not included in the budget. Therefore, the 'possessions' budgets include an element for the child's share of the cost of a colour television and television licence, again apportioned according to the mothers' decision, the total cost divided by the number of people living in the household.

Jackie (2) 'It's because they'll be picked on and feel left out. I mean, everybody has got a television, for a child to turn round in school and say, "I haven't got one", they're going to get pounced on straight away.'
6 – 10 years

Stationery and writing materials which need to be replaced more frequently than other possessions were dealt with by reaching a consensus on a minimum essential list of those items which children of different ages should have. Mothers then decided to allocate a weekly, monthly or annual figure for the purchase of paper, pens, glue and so on. For example, mothers in the two- to five-year age group allowed £1 per week for this.

An allowance for bedding has been calculated and included in the possessions budget. Mothers made decisions about the quantity of bedding required at any one time and the number of times bedding would need to be replaced during the years up to age 16.

BABY EQUIPMENT

Mothers reached consensus on a list of minimum essential items of baby equipment and were then asked to agree which items they felt could be used again, and which would only last for one child. They agreed that no items in this category could be used for more than two children and that items used once could be resold after one child for half their original value. Amounts included in the budget standard for these items therefore represent half their new cost.

ACTIVITIES

The budgets for activities include an allowance for certain school-based activities for the 6-10- and 11-16-year age groups, for mother and toddler, and for play group for the younger age groups.

Mothers also allowed for certain regular out of school activities and for irregular activities such as going to birthday parties, and a visit to Father Christmas. This area of the budget is more usually referred to as 'leisure' or 'entertainment', which carries connotations of luxury. The mothers felt strongly that the small number of activities for which they have allowed are absolutely essential to the proper development of the child.

Sally (2)   'It teaches them how to behave in public. It broadens their horizons as well ... and it also teaches them how much things cost ... you know, "you can't do it every week 'cause it's so expensive".'
             6 – 10 years

Dawn (2)   'It's the children's right ... If you don't give them the basic things for a start in life, you might as well forget it.'
             2 – 5 years

FURNITURE AND HOME DECORATING

Mothers agreed a list of minimum essential furnishings for the child's bedroom, and the number of times these would need to be replaced, if at all, during the 16-year period. The budget standard assumes that the child has her/his own bedroom from birth.

LAUNDRY

No allowance has been made in the budget for fuel costs (see below). Mothers allowed the family an automatic washing machine on the grounds that it is cheaper in the long run than going to a launderette once possible transport costs were also taken into account. They also indicated how many washes per week should be attributed to the child. Therefore, laundry costs include only an allowance for the total cost of the washing machine, plus the cost of soap powder.

TOILETRIES

This area of the budget includes allowances for bathing, hair washing, teeth cleaning, toilet rolls, towels and flannels for each age group at levels agreed by the mothers.

Good quality disposable nappies are included under this heading for the under-two-year and under-five-year age group; quality, quantities and length of time for which nappies are needed were again decided by the mothers.

For the older age group, mothers included an allowance for girls for good quality sanitary protection, hair remover and some cosmetics, and for both boys and girls for specialist skin cleansers, deodorant and talcum powder.

EXCLUSIONS FROM THE BUDGET STANDARD

Some comment is necessary on items of expenditure which occur in most family budgets but which have not been included in the budget standard.

TRANSPORT

The budget standards include no allowance for transport. Geographical differences in public transport costs, combined with their almost infinite variation according to the location of the home, meant that mothers were unable to agree a minimum essential figure for public transport. Only one of the groups felt that a car is an essential, although mothers felt that provision should be made to allow the child to get to school and to the activities for which they had allowed. They accepted that this might necessitate a car in rural areas.

HOUSING AND FUEL

No allowance for housing or fuel costs has been made in the budgets. Mothers agreed that housing should be adequate to allow boys and girls over the age of ten to have separate rooms. They decided that housing costs should be allocated to each child by taking total housing costs and dividing this by the number of people living in the household; that is, for a family of two adults and two children, the housing cost for one child would be one-quarter of the total housing costs.

Some form of heating was felt to be an essential minimum by the majority of mothers and, again, they agreed that fuel costs should be allocated to each child by taking total fuel costs and dividing by the number of people living in the household.

POCKET MONEY

The budget standards include no allowance for pocket money since no consensus emerged among mothers. However, they assumed that some of the items of expenditure included in their budgets would be paid for by the child from pocket money; for example, sweets, stationery and comics/hobby magazines.

THE BUDGET STANDARD AND INCOME SUPPORT RATES

The minimum essential budget standard described above represents parents' considered and agreed view of the absolute minimum which is required to bring up a child in Britain today. How does this compare to the actual amounts of money which parents on IS are given to bring up their children? Table 2 compares the parents' minimum budget standard for a child in each of the four age groups with IS rates plus family premium for 1994/95. For both calculations it is assumed that the child is living in a two-parent, two-child household. It should be borne in mind that the IS rates are for children aged under 11 years and between 11 and 15 years.

The table shows that the IS rate plus family premium would need to be increased by between 11 per cent and 56 per cent to meet the mothers' minimum essential budget. It seems that the needs of children between the ages of two and five years are the least likely to be met by IS. Weekly rates would need to be increased by £10.05 for a girl and £11.57 for a boy in order to meet the minimum budget agreed by mothers for this age group.

TABLE 2: **The budget standard and income support rates**

	Parents' minimum essential budget £	IS plus family premium £	Percentage difference[1] %	Shortfall £s[4]
Under 2 years:				
Girl	26.49	20.68[2]	− 28	5.81
Boy	26.33		− 27	5.65
2–5 years:				
Girl	30.73	20.68[2]	− 49	10.05
Boy	32.25		− 56	11.57
6–10 years:				
Girl	28.12	20.68[2]	− 36	7.44
Boy	27.67		− 34	6.99
11–16 years:				
Girl	31.04	28.03[3]	− 11	3.01
Boy	31.09		− 11	3.06

1. Percentage difference between IS plus family premium and parents' minimum essential budget.
2. Child aged under 11 years.
3. Child aged 11–15 years.
4. Difference in £s between IS plus family premium and parents' minimum essential budget.

A detailed comparison of the parents' minimum essential budgets with the low-cost budgets for children produced by Oldfield and Yu is not possible here. However, it is worth noting that their budget for a child aged under 11 years represented an average shortfall of £5.74 per week compared to an average shortfall of £7.92 for parents' minimum essential budgets.[5]

SOCIETY'S SUPPORT FOR CHILDREN

In constructing their lists of minimum essential items, mothers in the initial groups were not asked to consider the monetary cost of the items which they included. Rather, they concentrated on the things to which they felt every child should have the right as an absolute minimum.

Therefore, comparisons between the parents' minimum essential budget standards and IS levels could be open to criticism on the grounds that parents do not have to concern themselves with the financial implications of their budgets. Financial support for children is only one element of the total social security budget which, in turn, represents just one of the competing demands of a number of government departments on a finite national budget.

We decided to introduce a financial element into parents' thinking during the final set of groups. Parents were told the approximate weekly cost of the lists which they had agreed for each budget area and for their total budget. They were then asked to imagine that the group facilitator was the Chancellor of the Exchequer. They had come with their list to be told that the country could not afford to ensure that every child had all the items on that list. They were asked how they would respond and if they would agree to reduce their list. This approach was adopted for each list in turn and, finally, for their total budget.

It was anticipated that mothers would, at this stage, agree to reduce their lists in the light of this financial constraint. This proved not to be the case. Mothers from all social backgrounds refused to consider reducing any of their lists of essential items, stating firmly that these were an absolute minimum which no child should have to do without. They felt that their lists were already far from generous, in many cases expressing surprise at the low weekly cost of their budgets.

Jacqueline (3)   'I mean it's not as if you're asking for any luxuries for them. Unless you want them to walk barefooted or go cold in the winter or whatever, I mean, they're bare essentials ... so I mean, it's up to him to find the money, they deserve at least that.'

                Under 2 years

Laura (3)   [On the food budget] 'God, that's cheap isn't it?'

Sally (2)   'That's less than I thought it would be though. I thought it was going to be a lot more.'

Ann (2)   'I thought it would be dearer than that, yeah, a helluva lot more.'

                6 – 10 years

Children were considered to be the absolute and overriding priority in the allocation of the national budget.

Julie (1)   'To give mine or any other child the opportunity, the children of this nation to become decent adults.'

Sally (2)   'That's right, they've got to look at it as an investment in the future. He would invest in, I don't know, British Telecom ... But they won't invest in the children's future. And I think the children's future is more important than a telephone.'

6 – 10 years

Mothers also expressed disquiet at the extent of inequalities in the lifestyles of children which they saw around them.

Alice (1) 'There's a lot of things if you're living on a bare minimum – it must be really heartbreaking to know that your child has got the right to try out things – be it music, be it cycling, etc, etc – but you can't possibly afford it. And it's getting that there's more and more families like that, isn't there, that they want to give their children opportunities but they just can't afford to do it.'

11 – 16 years

Adrienne (2) [Talking about a friend who is living on benefit] 'What upsets me about their predicament is her children seem cut off from a lot of activities that other children take part in as a matter of course, and they feel themselves excluded ... the difference in lifestyle between people with money and the lifestyle without is huge.'

6 – 16 years

In conclusion, mothers were unimpressed by the idea that their minimum budget for children in 1994 in Britain could not be afforded. They were depressed by the thought that their own children might have to survive on the budget which they had drawn up. Furthermore, they were insistent that a successful future is dependent on ensuring that all children have access at the very least to the things included in their minimum essential budget.

Adrienne (2) 'I think people should look at all children as assets for the future, whoever they belong to, and make sure that they are looked after, provided for. They are our future aren't they? When we're pensioners, they'll be paying for us.'

6 – 16 years

Yet the shortfalls between the budget standard and IS rates show that many children in Britain experience living standards which parents believe guarantee their exclusion from society and severely restrict their chances of reaching anything like their full potential.

The weekly monetary amounts involved are relatively small, in line with the findings of other research, which has also shown that a very little extra money makes a great deal of difference to the lives of people on low incomes.[6] However, the cumulative impact of the shortfall as children grow up must be severe.

NOTES

1. J Bradshaw, *Household Budgets and Living Standards*, Joseph Rowntree Foundation, 1993.
2. N Oldfield and A S Yu, *The Cost of a Child: living standards for the 1990s*, Child Poverty Action Group, 1993.
3. A more detailed report of this work will be published by the Joseph Rowntree Foundation in early 1995.
4. A fuller description of the recruitment and make-up of the groups can be found in the Appendix.
5. Oldfield and Yu, *op cit*, p57.
6. E Kempson, A Bryson and K Rawlingson, *Hard Times: how poor families make ends meet*, Policy Studies Institute, 1994. B Dobson, A Beardsworth, T Keil, R Walker, *Diet, Choice and Poverty*, Family Policy Studies Centre (forthcoming).

2

'Reeboks, a Game Boy and a cat': things children own

Karl Ashworth, Sue Middleton, Robert Walker, Karen Kellard, Anne Peaker and Michelle Thomas

INTRODUCTION

As adults we surround ourselves with possessions. Ownership of the latest car, washing machine and compact disc player seem for many of us to be badges of social acceptability which we display to the outside world and by which we judge others. In 1990s Britain we are what we own. At the same time, however, we criticise children for displaying the same acquisitive tendencies. Their demands for the latest computer games, designer training shoes and video machines (VCRs) are said to indicate an unhealthy materialism which, in turn, is blamed for the supposed failings of the younger generation.

Yet possessions may play a similar role in the lives of children as they do for adults, serving as passports into the world of friends, as badges of confidence and to secure peer approval. Since we know that it is largely through play and social participation that children prepare for independence in the adult world, possessions which enable such participation may be crucial to a child's social development. Conversely, failure to own certain things may result in exclusion from the social world of their peers. For example, Chapter Four illustrates the exclusion, embarrassment and even abuse that can result when children do not have the 'expected' clothing. Therefore children, as much as and perhaps even more than adults, are often under pressure to have particular possessions, without which it is difficult for them to either 'do' or 'be' certain things. This pressure on children is then translated into financial demands on parents and others, so that an understanding of the things children have, and the things children want to have, is crucial to our exploration of the pressures on parents.

However, children's ownership ambitions are unlikely to be built entirely upon what others have. Children vary as much as adults in their tastes and interests and in their desire to be part of social groups. Some of these differences will be related to age, sex and socio-economic background, which in turn reflect the more complex factors influencing children's aspirations. Children may want to own certain things, even though they are aware that their parents would never agree to buy them or, indeed, could not afford them. Equally, some children may deny themselves such aspirations because they know their parents' finances are limited.

This chapter explores the material world of children. It examines the things which children have, their favourite things and the things which they would like to have.

THINGS CHILDREN HAVE

The children to whom we talked were given a limited amount of time to list the things they owned. More than 300 different possessions were mentioned, ranging from expensive consumer durables, such as audio and visual equipment and computers and games machines, to stationery and hair-bobbles.

Toys were most frequently listed, mentioned by 90 per cent of the children. Clothes came next, listed by 78 per cent. Clearly, we cannot deduce from the previous figure that 22 per cent of children have no clothes of their own, since children did not have time to think of all the things which they own. However, it is striking how many children thought to list electronic consumer goods. Sixty-eight per cent said they had some audio equipment, 62 per cent a computer or games machine of some kind, 51 per cent a television and 21 per cent a video. When asked directly about their ownership of electronic home entertainment items – or access to them as main user – the percentages were even greater.

The similarity between the possessions owned by children from the more and less affluent areas shown in Figure 2.1 is striking. It is clear that children have the same things whatever their socio-economic background. A common culture of acquisition exists among children which must place disproportionately greater demands on the family budgets of less affluent parents.

In particular, children's access to electrical consumer goods differed

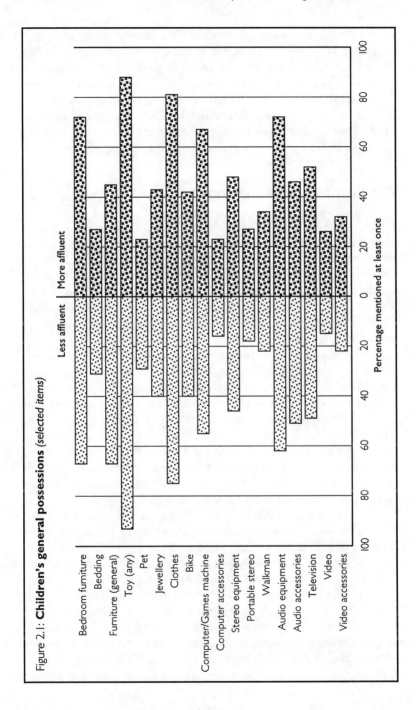

Figure 2.1: **Children's general possessions** (selected items)

little between the more affluent and less affluent areas. Indeed, if anything, ownership of, or access to, such goods was slightly higher among less affluent children. In addition, purchase of such items as VCRs and computers can generate further demands for accessories, cartridges and the like, which are often disproportionately expensive.

It seems that poorer parents must be making sacrifices in other areas of the family budget in order to satisfy or placate their children's demands, an issue which we explore further in Chapter Nine.

CHILDREN'S FAVOURITE THINGS

Children were also asked to list their favourite possessions. Again, a wide range of items were mentioned, some of which were mentioned by only a few children. Figure 2.2 lists only those things which were described as favourite by a fifth, or more, of the children. Three of the four most favourite items were, again, home consumer goods: audio equipment, computers and televisions; clothes were the fourth. Each of these items was listed at least once by between 40 and 50 per cent of children.

While children from all socio-economic backgrounds ranked electronic goods high in their list of favourite possessions, there were some subtle differences of emphasis. For example, children from more affluent families were more likely to list audio equipment and television as a favourite possession than were their less affluent counterparts. The differences (21 and 15 per cent, respectively) exceed differences in the level of ownership of these items between the two groups and therefore suggest real differences in the degree of attachment to such items. It is worth noting that not every child who owned a television included it in their list of favourite possessions.[1]

The children also differed in the number and type of possessions which they listed as their favourite. Although listing the same average number of possessions overall, children from more affluent families listed on average 5.8 favourite possessions compared to only 4.4 listed by those from less affluent families. The explanation for this is unclear, but may be a product of the limited time which children were given to list the things which they owned. The more affluent children might have included fewer of their total stock of possessions than less affluent children, in which case the latter would have a smaller number of possessions from which to select favourites, thus leading them to list fewer favourites. On the other hand, it may be that the general

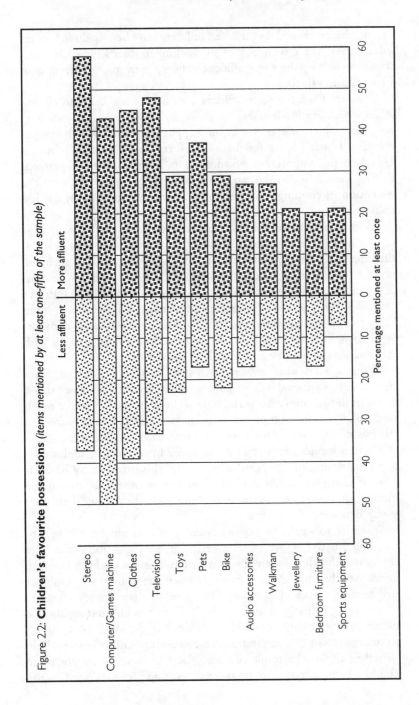

Figure 2.2: **Children's favourite possessions** (items mentioned by at least one-fifth of the sample)

list of things owned by the less affluent children included items which they had grown out of or no longer valued, whereas those things owned by the more affluent children were more current and, hence, more valued.

Children from the more affluent area were more likely to choose items which can be described as having 'symbolic' value, for example: jewellery, which relates to personal appearance; pets, which suggest emotional attachment; and bedroom furnishings, which Furby has linked to the importance of adolescents having space for personal development.[2] In contrast, no items of 'symbolic' relevance, with the exception of clothing, were listed by as many as one-fifth of the less affluent children.

Clothes are important to children irrespective of their socio-economic background and seem to become ever more significant as they get older. Seventy-six per cent of 15- to 16-year-olds included at least one item of clothing among their favourite possessions compared with 54 per cent of 12- to 13-year-olds and just four per cent of seven-year olds. Moreover, the younger children were more likely to cite practical reasons for liking their clothes, such as comfort, whereas older ones were more likely to mention factors to do with self-image, such as 'they make me look good'.

While clothes were important to both boys and girls, girls were more likely to include them among their favourite possessions (48 per cent did so compared with 38 per cent of boys). Boys were much more likely to list computers as favourites; computers appeared on the lists of seven out of ten boys compared with two out of ten girls.

Clothes would seem to take on an added importance in adolescence as an expression of emerging self-identity. This process may be inhibited if teenagers cannot, for lack of money or other reasons, buy the clothes they want or, as Chapter Four will show, that their peer group demands.

In order to begin to explore sources of pressure on children to own certain things, we asked a series of questions about why the things they had listed were their favourites. These included a question about whether any of their friends owned the same thing. Only 21 per cent of the children stated that none of their friends owned a similar thing to the one which s/he had listed, with most saying that either a few or many of their friends also had the same thing. Again, a common culture of acquisition can be seen to exist among children. Whether this is the result of peer group pressure or simply of all children being exposed to the same advertising pressures (see Chapter

Six) is unclear. However, whereas 31 per cent of the more affluent children said that many/all of their friends owned a similar object, only 21 per cent of children from less affluent families said the same and this may be an indication of their inability to participate in the common culture of acquisition.

However, when asked spontaneously, in general the children gave simple practical reasons for choosing things as favourite: 'I just like riding my bike', or 'it stops me from getting bored'. Elaboration on this theme related to the use, or variety of uses, to which a thing could be put, VCRs play videos, computers play games, and so on, and its appearance, 'I like the colour'. One in four of the children, mainly those who had chosen 'symbolic' items such as pets, or family members as favourite, gave emotional reasons, such as 'because I like to cuddle them', or 'because I love them'. This was most common among the young adolescent (the 12- to 13-year-old) children, 41 per cent of whom gave such reasons.

Favourite possessions had mainly been received as presents (73 per cent) and 45 per cent of the children said that they had asked for them. However, again there were differences by socio-economic background. Eighty-three per cent of children from less affluent families had been given their favourite thing as a present, compared with only 67 per cent of the more affluent children. The children from more affluent families were also much more likely to have asked for their most favourite possession (50 per cent compared with only 30 per cent of less affluent children).

It seems, therefore, that children from higher income families are less dependent upon presents as a source of valued items but, when they do get presents, have a greater say in what they want. Their friends are also more likely to own similar favourite things than their less affluent peers.

THINGS CHILDREN WOULD LIKE TO OWN

So far in this chapter we have seen the kind of things that children own and value. What things do they still long for? The answer appears to be more of the same.

Knowledge of children's favourite things is important for an understanding of the things that they want. Ownership of one of some items will usually be enough to satisfy a child's desires, for example, children can presumably only watch one television at once!

However, as mentioned above, things such as computers, stereos and VCRs often act as a platform for the desire for further purchases. Children might also want improved versions of an item which they already own, such as computers. They also grow out of certain things, such as bikes, and may want a replacement. Therefore, what children want may be related to what they already have.

The children were asked to list the things they would ask for 'if it was their birthday next week'. Clothes were mentioned most frequently, followed by computers and computer accessories, such as games, joysticks and control-pads, etc, and, primarily among older children, money. Ownership of some things, notably computers, but also 'collectibles' such as Barbie dolls and Sylvanian families, does indeed seem to stimulate demands for other, usually better and more expensive, items.

Children tended to want on average marginally fewer items than they listed as favourites (4.5 compared with 5.3). However, there was no statistically significant difference between the average lengths of the 'wish lists' of the more and less affluent groups of children. This suggests that the demands likely to be placed on parents at their child's next birthday are unlikely to be much less for poorer families than for more affluent ones.

Computers and computer accessories, money and clothes were equally likely to appear on the wanted lists of children from both lower and higher income families. Children from more affluent backgrounds also often wanted musical equipment and accessories such as tapes, records and compact discs; and, perhaps again reflecting a greater attachment to 'symbolic' things, pets and jewellery. However, 'traditional' items such as a bike and toys, which were included on the lists of favourite things by children from both socio-economic backgrounds, only appeared on the 'wish lists' of the less affluent children. This may be because children from affluent homes feel that they already have adequate stocks of such things, whereas children from poorer households do not.

The children were asked to choose the item on their list that they wanted most of all and, again, were questioned further about it. Reasons given for wanting an item were similar to those for choosing something as favourite. However, the children also introduced the concept of need, either the 'need' to replace something which they had outgrown, or the 'need' to improve on something which they already had.

Although the fact that friends already owned a wanted item did

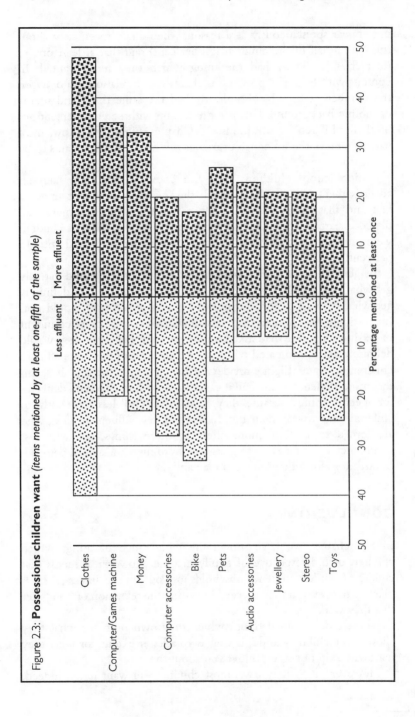

Figure 2.3: **Possessions children want** (items mentioned by at least one-fifth of the sample)

not appear spontaneously as a reason, when asked specifically about this over a half of the children (55 per cent) said that at least one of their friends already had the thing which they most wanted. In contrast with favourite possessions, there was no relationship between the number of friends who already had the same thing and socio-economic background. This is more in line with parents' perceptions of their children's motivations. As Chapter Eight will show, most parents believe the influence of friends on their children's wants to be very great indeed.

Junior school children were also asked if they had seen an advertisement for the thing which they wanted most. Just under a half said that they had and, when asked if the advertisement had played a part in their desire for the item, the less affluent children were more likely to admit that it had (68 per cent compared with 45 per cent).

In general the children were optimistic that they would actually get what they want. Fifty-one per cent thought they would definitely get what they asked for, and only 11 per cent said they would not. Interestingly, the children from less affluent areas were more confident of getting what they had asked for, 67 per cent believing they would definitely get it, compared with only 42 per cent of the more affluent children. Chapter Eight provides further evidence for this. It seems that more affluent parents find it easier to resist their children's demands for specific things because they have to say 'no' less frequently to children's day-to-day demands. In contrast, less affluent parents, who are forced to say 'no' more often, to more things, but with less consistency, presumably go to great lengths to meet the annual demands of birthdays, for which they can plan and save.

CONCLUSION

In this chapter we have shown the wide range of things which children own, irrespective of family income. However, it seems that children from less affluent households lose out on the 'basics', such as bikes or toys, even if they succeed in getting the television or computer that they want.

The children valued things which they own both for what they allowed the children to do, as well as, to a lesser extent, for what they felt ownership of certain things said about them.

However much they have, most children still want more. Indeed, certain items such as computers and 'collectibles' are designed with a view to creating further demand, and we have shown that advertising did have an effect, at least on the junior school children. In addition to advertising, it is clear that children are influenced by what their friends have.

The remarkable similarities between children from different socio-economic backgrounds with respect to the things which they own and want to own suggest that a common culture of acquisition exists among children. These wants, as we shall see later, translate into financial demands on parents which all find hard to resist, but which, inevitably, fall disproportionately on the budgets of less well-off families.

NOTES

1. Children were not asked if items were owned or rented.
2. L Furby, 'Possession in humans: an exploratory study of its meaning and motivation', *Social Behaviour and Personality*, 6 (1), 1978, pp49-65.

3 'There's nothing to do round here': things children do

Karl Ashworth, Sue Middleton, Robert Walker, Karen Kellard, Anne Peaker and Michelle Thomas

Chapter One has shown that children value some of the things which they have and want because they allow them to take part in particular activities. However, children also participate in activities which, whilst not dependent on owning expensive possessions, still carry a financial cost for the family, such as swimming, holidays, going to birthday parties. While the activities will vary to some extent with individual preferences, cost inevitably limits both the type and range for children in most families. In this chapter we explore the activities in which children participate and how these vary with economic circumstances, as well as with age and gender.

However, the fact that a child regularly takes part in an activity does not necessarily mean that this is her/his favourite activity. It may be, for example, that there are other things which the child would prefer to do but which the family cannot afford. Therefore, this chapter goes on to describe both children's favourite activities and the activities which they would like to be able to do.

WHAT CHILDREN DO

Children do a very wide range of things in their spare time and these vary by age and gender. In addition, children vary in their ability to describe these activities. The individual diaries of the four children below were chosen because they were typical of their gender and age group and highlight the similarities and differences between their activities.

Boys and girls did similar things. The youngest children often played at or around the home, in the street or the garden, or in the house itself. Many went to visit, or were visited by, relatives at weekends and often accompanied parents on shopping trips. Whilst this general pattern of activity continued for the older junior school children, they were apparently granted more freedom. For example, 10- and 11-year-olds reported going out cycling with their friends and were allowed to play further from home, in public parks and recreation grounds.

A number of differences were apparent between children from different socio-economic backgrounds. For example, children from less affluent backgrounds were more likely to have a greater degree of freedom at age six or seven, although this difference began to disappear by the time they were ten or eleven. Children from more affluent families were more likely to play with construction toys such as Lego, and more likely to belong to the Cubs/Brownies or Scouts/Guides. These children were also more likely to play musical instruments and to receive both school-based and private tuition. In contrast, the few children from less affluent backgrounds who did play a musical instrument were largely dependent on school-based tuition.

Sports were popular with most children. However, with the exception of football, it was again the children from better-off families who were more likely to be involved in school, or externally organised, clubs. This was most apparent at the age of ten to eleven. Moreover, while football and swimming were popular irrespective of sex, age and socio-economic background, other games (eg, tennis), were usually played only by children from more affluent homes. The range of activities appeared to be somewhat greater for children from more affluent neighbourhoods and their days were generally more structured.

Children spent a lot of their time watching television and videos, playing on computers and listening to music. Television, in particular, played a large part in nearly all children's lives and this is further described below. It was mainly boys who reported playing often with their computer. This confirms the findings of previous research by Murdock *et al* which showed that only one in seven households with computers reported that the main user was female.[1] However, despite the fact that children from both socio-economic backgrounds were almost equally as likely to describe their computer as a favourite possession (see Chapter Two), boys from less affluent families were less likely to report actually playing on their computers, again confirming the findings of previous research.[2]

TABLE 1: **Activity reports of junior school children**

More affluent, age 7-8 years boy	Less affluent, age 7-8 years girl
Activities undertaken the previous night Went home after school. Played in the back garden with sister and mother. Then I had tea. Then I watched telly. Then I went to bed. *Regular activities* Football (local team member). Trying to get into a cricket team but can't find one. I used to be in the Cubs but gave up because everyone bossed me around. Guitar in school – I'm going to get one to play at home.	*Activities undertaken the previous night* Played out with my friend. Watched telly. Had my tea. Did hand-stands. Went to shop. Had a cup of tea. Played out again with my friend and sister. Slept at my Nan's. *Regular activities* I used to go to gymnastics but we packed it in because my Aunty couldn't keep taking us. When it's a real hot day my Dad takes me swimming. Sometimes I go up to the rec and play on the swings and that.

More affluent, age 10-11 girl	Less affluent, age 10-11 boy
Activities undertaken the previous night Went to town shopping with my Mum at Sainsbury's. Went back home and sat in front of television. Ate biscuits. Looked at list of things to do. Did homework. Did diary. Practised violin – my Dad played the piano with me. Played a bit. Tidied up my room. Had dinner. Went to bed. *Regular activities* Swimming every Wednesday. Violin. I was in a tennis club but I gave that up. There's probably loads of things I've done but I can't remember them now.	*Activities undertaken the previous night* Had my tea. Played football with friend and his brother. Watched television. Went out on the streets then in the woods. Went in and played on computer. Watched television. Went to bed about 10.00pm. *Regular activities* Karate. Football (school team as well as with friends). Swimming at Leisure Centre – my Mum and Dad drop us on a Saturday and pick us up on the way back. Canoeing at the club.

Ballet, dance and drama were mentioned by a number of girls, mainly at age ten to eleven. School-based organisations offered the children from less affluent families the opportunity to participate in these with, again, children from more affluent families having both school and private tuition.

The activities of secondary school children showed considerable variation by gender and age. The 12- to 13-year-old boys did many of the same things as the 10- to 11-year-olds, namely football, television and computers. However, freedom of movement had increased further by this age; they were often out and playing games such as 'fox and hounds', 'tiggy' and hide-and-seek. Less affluent boys mentioned 'hanging about on the streets' more often than did their better-off counterparts, who were more likely to describe going round to a friend's home as a part of their usual round of activities.

The 12- and 13-year-old boys knew of young people, both in school and outside school, who were involved in theft and drug use. Most knew where they could obtain drugs, and a number of the less affluent boys said they had tried drugs, whilst none of the more affluent boys admitted to this. However, some had tried cigarettes and also believed that cannabis is 'better for you' than cigarettes.

At the age of 15 or 16 television, the computer and homework were all mentioned as regular activities, although homework was of less concern to the less affluent young men. This was paralleled by a lack of ambition in describing their post-school aspirations. The less affluent group were less likely to perceive themselves as being able to get a job but were, at the same time, much less likely to think about further education than their more affluent counterparts.

The better-off young people in this age group tended to be anti-crime in general, although the use of cannabis was condoned, and some admitted to using it fairly regularly. While denying their own involvement, the more affluent young men reported that 'thieving' was quite often done by some of their peers, both male and female, for the 'kicks' arising from the risk of getting caught, rather than for financial gain.

David   'Like a lot of the kids that thieve and that, everyone thinks they're from down [a less affluent area] ... but it's very rare now that you get any petty thieves from places like that. Usually from places like [a more affluent area] where they've got money and it's like a bit of a challenge to 'em. Like their parents are doctors and they say, "Don't do this and do that and sit in and do this", and they go down and discover cigarettes and booze and drugs and thieving and stuff like that... Oh, yeah, I did something behind my Mum's back, she's never going to find out about me, I'm doing something that's making me look a bit better. I'm not that simple person any more.'

MA, M, 15 years

Their less affluent peers tended to be less generally anti-crime, with one admitting to having himself been involved in both theft and joyriding:

Sam   'I trust me mates who I know. I wouldn't go with someone I didn't know who was a joyrider like, just go with me mates. It's quite fun sometimes.'

LA, M, 16 years

However, it must be emphasised that those involved in drugs and crime were a very small minority among this age group.

Pubs had also started to exercise a fascination for young men in this age group and a small number from both socio-economic backgrounds reported going into them on a fairly regular basis. Although the cost was seen as relatively prohibitive if the aim was to get drunk, visits to pubs were, fortunately, seen more as social occasions!

Girls and young women reported some quite different activities and concerns from the boys and young men. Both of the older age groups, from both socio-economic backgrounds, often visited their friends to chat and listen to music. They were much less likely to 'hang around on the streets' and this pastime declined even further with age, irrespective of socio-economic background. As with the boys, sport was still relatively popular with girls aged 12 to 13 years, although the more affluent girls were more likely to say they had been horse-riding than their less affluent counterparts. Further, the popularity of sport had again declined among the 15- to 16-year-old young women, as socialising increasingly revolved around 'visiting each other' and 'going into town shopping'.

Girls were less likely to admit both to crime and knowledge of crime than were their male colleagues. They were also generally anti-crime and, although they also knew where they could get drugs, were less likely to have tried them. These young people were therefore typical of their age group. It is known that boys are far more likely to offend than girls. In particular, boys in the 10–16-year age group are seven times more likely than girls to have been found guilty or cautioned for drugs offences.[3] Quite a number of the older girls reported that they went to pubs and clubs, more for social reasons than for access to alcohol, although they said that they would drink alcohol if they could afford to.

SPECIFIC ACTIVITIES

Children were asked a series of supplementary questions about television, reading and holidays. Television and reading were chosen for particular attention as relatively frequent activities which represent opposite sides of the coin in terms of popular perceptions of children and the way in which they spend their time. Children watching too much of the 'wrong sort' of television is often blamed for a range of social ills, from declining educational standards to juvenile crime. Conversely, children reading less or, indeed, not reading at all, is said to be equally responsible for the same social ills. In contrast, holidays were included because they are a relatively expensive but infrequent activity, which we anticipated might suggest interesting variations in the experiences of children from different socio-economic backgrounds.

TELEVISION

Virtually all the children reported that they had watched some television the night before the interview (98 per cent). The older children were also asked how many hours they normally spent watching television in an evening: 51 per cent stated that they had watched for two hours or more. Furthermore, 50 per cent of those who said they watched television for an hour or less stated that this was less than usual, in comparison with only 31 per cent of those watching for three hours or more who said that this was more than usual.

Evidence suggests that the extent of television viewing by children is strongly related to social class. For example, *Social Focus on Children* shows that children in social classes D and E watch on average five hours per week more television than those in social classes A and B.[4] The children in this study were no exception. Thirty-three per cent of children from less affluent neighbourhoods reported watching for three hours or more – over twice as many as their counterparts from more affluent families. This difference possibly echoes the finding above that children from higher status neighbourhoods tend to have more structure to their leisure time which might, in turn, reflect differences in family attitudes about how that time is spent. However, it is also likely that children from less affluent backgrounds watch more television because it is a relatively cheap and accessible form of entertainment, compared with the wider range of more expensive activities to which more affluent children have access.

Children were also asked both about the programmes which they had watched the previous night and about programmes which they watch regularly. Soap operas were the most watched group of programmes, both on the previous night and for regular viewing, again showing the extent to which these children were typical of their age group.[5] Forty-six per cent of children had watched at least one soap the night before the interview, but 65 per cent claimed to watch at least one regularly. No other type of programme was as popular as the soaps. Adult drama was watched regularly by 15 per cent of children and, on the previous night, by 20 per cent. Other relatively popular programmes were cartoons, police series, comedy and children's television in general.

It is interesting that one programme – one in a series of films about magic and hypnosis – was watched by 13 per cent of children on the previous night but was said to be regularly watched by only three per cent. A similar effect occurs for news, documentaries and drama programmes. This difference between what was actually watched the night before and what children watch regularly (presumably those programmes they like best), is probably caused by a combination of casual viewing, watching what happens to be on and, perhaps, parental choices of viewing taking priority over the children's likes and dislikes.

It is clear that these children use television primarily as a means of entertainment and not as a source of knowledge and information about the world around them. No children reported watching science/ nature programmes on a regular basis, and only five per cent regularly watched the news. However, more children reported having actually watched these programmes the night before. This suggests that imbedding such programmes between other, more popular, programmes does increase the number of children who will watch them.

Few differences in programme popularity emerged between children from different socio-economic backgrounds. Soaps were equally popular for both groups of children and, conversely, educational programmes were equally unpopular. However, 5 per cent of the children from more affluent neighbourhoods did regularly watch the news, compared with none of their less affluent counterparts who were more likely to watch cartoons (mainly the youngest children) and police series. Children from more affluent neighbourhoods were also more inclined to watch dramas.

It would be easy to conclude from this that children are indeed watching 'too much' of the 'wrong sort' of television. However, two notes of caution should be sounded. First, few of the children reported that watching television was a favourite activity of theirs, expressing preferences for doing other things whenever possible. Second, evidence from parents who filled in an activity diary on one of their children suggests that children do not watch television in long uninterrupted sessions. Analysis of the activity diaries, which were divided into one-hour slots, indicates that children dip in and out of television and/or are often doing other things while the television is on in the background. This confirms the findings of previous research which has also shown that television often provides a background to other activities and that, in fact, many adolescents would be happy to watch less television.[6]

READING

Evidence about the relationship between the extent of television viewing and frequency of reading is inconclusive. Research by Medrich *et al* indicates a strong inverse relationship between television use and reading.[7] However, although the children in our study spent a significant amount of time watching television, this was by no means to the total exclusion of reading. Indeed, Neumann found only a slight negative association between the extent of television viewing and frequency of reading.[8] While fewer children read on the previous night than watched television (59 per cent compared with 98 per cent), over half of each age group stated that they had read something, with the 10- to 11-year-old children, girls and children from more affluent neighbourhoods being the most likely to have read.

Junior school children had mostly read books (69 per cent of those who had read), as opposed to newspapers or magazines. However, it is interesting that the children from less affluent neighbourhoods were more likely to have read a book (91 per cent) than those from more affluent neighbourhoods (56 per cent). This may provide supportive evidence for earlier research which suggests that, whilst increased television viewing is associated with less frequent reading, it tends to be the reading of material such as comics which is displaced.

Conversely, the reading of what the research describes as 'quality' materials increases with higher levels of television viewing.[9]

Children were also asked about how often their parents read to them. Contrary to conventional wisdom, the parents of more affluent children were less likely to read regularly or occasionally to their children than the parents in less affluent neighbourhoods. This contradicts previous research which has consistently shown that better-off parents adopt a more active role in many aspects of their children's education, including reading, than their less affluent counterparts.[10] We can only speculate on the reason for this contradiction. It may be that asking this question in a school environment which encouraged children to get their parents to read to them, caused the less affluent children to exaggerate the extent to which their parents read to them. The less affluent children might also be less skilled readers than their more affluent colleagues who, therefore, do not need their parents to read to them.

The secondary school children were also asked about the length of time they had spent reading and about their use of public libraries. Of the 56 per cent of those children who had read the night before, the majority had read for less than one hour (68 per cent). However, 26 per cent said that this was less than they usually read, compared with only 8 per cent who said this was more than usual. Children from more affluent families in these older age groups were as likely to have a read a book on the previous night as their less affluent counterparts, but were more likely to have read for longer. However, the children from more affluent families were also more likely to say that the amount of time which they had spent reading was more than usual, whereas those from less affluent neighbourhoods were more likely to claim that they had read for less time than was usual.

Most of the secondary school children used a public library at some time (62 per cent), although a quarter used it less frequently than once a month. Children from higher socio-economic backgrounds used the library more often than their less affluent peers.

Although it is undeniable that these children spent more time watching television than reading, reading is by no means the lost cause for this generation of children that some pundits would have us believe. Children are still reading, and being read to, regularly and make use of public libraries. Further, there is little conclusive evidence to suggest that reading is any less common an activity among less affluent children.

HOLIDAYS

Children were asked a series of questions about any holidays which they had taken in the previous 12 months. The majority of holidays which they described were at places within the British Isles or Ireland (62 per cent), and the majority had been of one week or less (46 per cent); a further 23 per cent had had a holiday of up to two weeks.

However, striking differences emerged between the holiday experiences of children from different socio-economic backgrounds. As Figure 3.1 shows, children from more affluent families were more likely to have spent their holiday in Europe or in other continents. Further, they were also likely to stay for longer: about twice as many children from more affluent neighbourhoods had holidays of longer than one week, than did their counterparts from less affluent backgrounds (Figure 3.2).

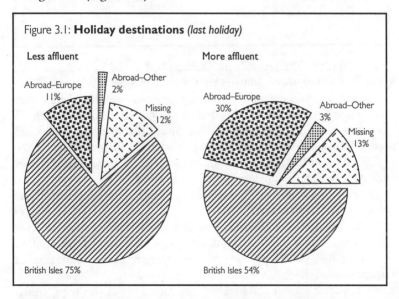

Figure 3.1: **Holiday destinations** *(last holiday)*

Less affluent

Abroad–Europe 11%
Abroad–Other 2%
Missing 12%
British Isles 75%

More affluent

Abroad–Europe 30%
Abroad–Other 3%
Missing 13%
British Isles 54%

The type of accommodation in which the holiday was spent also differed significantly. Children from less affluent neighbourhoods were about three times more likely to have stayed in a caravan, about five times more likely to have stayed in a tent, and twice as likely to have stayed at a relative's house, than children from more affluent families. In contrast, children from more affluent backgrounds were about five times more likely to have stayed in a cottage, with 7 per cent having spent their holiday in a villa and the same percentage in a friend's

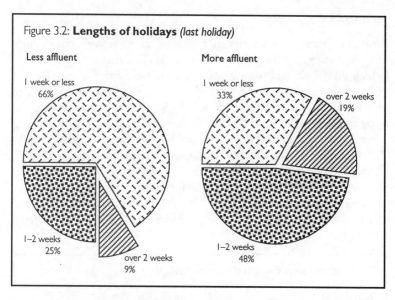

Figure 3.2: **Lengths of holidays** (last holiday)

Less affluent — More affluent

Less affluent: 1 week or less 66%; 1–2 weeks 25%; over 2 weeks 9%

More affluent: 1 week or less 33%; over 2 weeks 19%; 1–2 weeks 48%

house. None of the less affluent children had stayed in a villa or with friends. Further, more affluent children were more likely to holiday in places which were new to them. Forty per cent stated that they had never been to the holiday destination before, compared with 25 per cent of less affluent children. The more affluent children also had more holidays – they were 50 per cent more likely to have three holidays a year than children from less affluent families. These findings are typical. For example, evidence from *Social Trends* shows that the higher social classes have more holidays, more frequently, than those in the lower social classes.[11]

The junior school children were also asked whether they had ever been abroad for a holiday or not. Overall, 47 per cent of the children said they had, but 81 per cent of these were from the more affluent neighbourhood.

The junior school children had also talked about day trips, which the less affluent children often defined as 'holidays'. Day trips were therefore discussed in greater detail with the secondary school children and, again, children's experiences varied according to their socio-economic background. Children from less affluent backgrounds were much more dependent on school for day trips, whereas children from more affluent homes received more trips from family and friends (Figure 3.3). Moreover, while children from the more affluent backgrounds were slightly less likely to go on day trips at all, when they went, they were more likely to go on two or three a year (Figure 3.4).

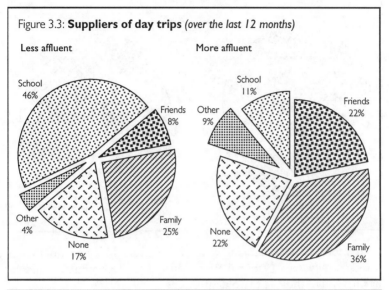

Figure 3.3: **Suppliers of day trips** *(over the last 12 months)*

Less affluent — More affluent

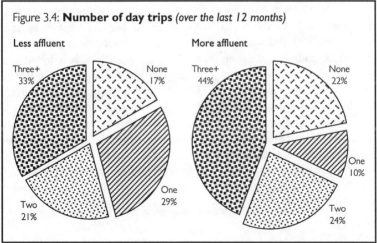

Figure 3.4: **Number of day trips** *(over the last 12 months)*

Less affluent — More affluent

There were also noticeable differences in destinations for day trips (Figure 3.5). Children from less affluent neighbourhoods were over three times more likely to go to a theme park, and six times more likely to go to a country park or stately home. In contrast, children

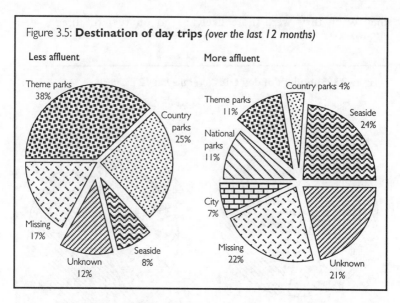

Figure 3.5: **Destination of day trips** *(over the last 12 months)*

Less affluent — More affluent

Less affluent:
Theme parks 38%
Country parks 25%
Seaside 8%
Unknown 12%
Missing 17%

More affluent:
Country parks 4%
Theme parks 11%
National parks 11%
Seaside 24%
City 7%
Missing 22%
Unknown 21%

from more affluent families were much more likely to go to the seaside, a city or a National Park; none of the less affluent children having visited these last two destinations.

It is clear that, for the less affluent children to whom we listened, the opportunities which holidays bring to broaden horizons and experience different environments are severely restricted. It can be argued, of course, that when family income is limited, it is inevitable that holidays and day trips are an unaffordable luxury. However, parents included an allowance for either day trips or a one-week holiday in Britain with the family in the minimum essential budgets described in Chapter One. The parents believe that it is very important for every child to be able to have at least some day trips or a one-week holiday away from home with his/her family every year. They see this as vital in cementing family relationships and broadening the child's horizons.

Marie (3) 'I think they need a holiday with the family...'
Dawn (2) 'Yeah.'
Marie (3) '...'cause that's the only time they can all be together as a family for a full week.'
Dawn (2) 'I would go without all the other things for a holiday.'
Marie (3) 'No one needs a holiday more than the kids these days.'
        2 – 5 years

The contrasting experiences of the children to whom we listened tend to confirm this view. For less affluent children the lack of access to day trips and holidays away from home is yet another contributory factor to their exclusion from the experiences of the majority of their peers.

Nicola   'Southport – it's a trip what I go on. Sometimes they take you to Skegness but when we went you had to get up right early to get the coach.'

Interviewer   'How long did you stay?'

Nicola   'The whole day.'

                LA, F, 7 years

Samantha   'France at Easter with Grandma and Granddad.'

Interviewer   'Have you been there before?'

Samantha   'Yes we go every year, twice a year. And then we go and stay with our other grandparents at bank holidays in England and with my aunt and uncle or we stay in hotels. At Christmas we stay at home. We go to other places on day trips. We go away for a long time in the big holidays like summer.'

Interviewer   'Where?'

Samantha   'Africa.'

                MA, F, 11 years

FAVOURITE ACTIVITIES

The activities which children do most are not necessarily their favourite activities. It has already been noted that whilst most children watch television, many do not describe this as a favourite activity. So, what do children enjoy doing most? The answer is that children are as individual in their leisure preferences as adults. They do not all favour spending all of their time playing computer games or listening to music. With the exception of sport, which was the favourite activity of nearly half the children, few children listed the same activity as favourite. Sport was a favourite with both socio-economic back-grounds, with boys and girls, and with all age groups. However, it was less popular with the 15- to 16-year-olds, dropping from being the favourite activity of 60 per cent of the 12- to13-year-olds to only 27 per cent of those aged 15 to 16 years.

Overall, it seems that socio-economic background has little bearing on what children actually like to spend their time doing. Children from both areas gave equally varied choices of favourite activities, except that none of the less affluent children included listening to music as a favourite activity, compared with 13 per cent of children from more affluent backgrounds. There was a slight tendency for the more affluent children to list more favourites than their less affluent counterparts. This parallels earlier findings that more affluent children have more favourite possessions and participate in a wider range of activities.

WHAT CHILDREN WOULD LIKE TO DO

Boys and girls from both areas bemoaned the lack of leisure facilities and the cost of those that were available to them. They discussed a range of things that they would like to do but could not through lack of money, such as Quasar, bowling and motorbike scrambling.

We also asked children to write a list of things they would like to be able to do. It might be anticipated that the frustrations of growing up in a family on a low income would emerge in these 'wish lists'. In addition, children from less affluent areas who presumably are less able to do what they would like to do because of lack of money, might be expected to produce longer lists than their more affluent peers. In the event, most of the children found it quite difficult to think of activities that they would most like to do. The activities listed most often were: 'white knuckle' sports, such as parachuting, bungee jumping, mountaineering, etc, mentioned by 21 per cent of children; and travel, mentioned by 18 per cent of children. This was in contrast to the more mundane activities which had emerged in earlier discussions.

The effect of the child's socio-economic background on what s/he would like to be able to do emerged somewhat differently from our expectations; the children from the less affluent neighbourhoods revealed limited aspirations. Children from more affluent neighbourhoods were five and a half times more likely to mention wanting to travel, usually the world or a specified part of it, than their less affluent peers. In contrast, the less affluent children were almost twice as likely to mention simply wanting to 'go on holiday'. In addition, wanting to go horse-riding was not mentioned by any of the less affluent children but was listed by nine per cent of the more affluent children. Twelve per cent of more affluent children also said they would like to meet 'someone famous', a concern which was not addressed at all by their less affluent counterparts. Whilst the possibility of this last desire being fulfilled is unlikely to be related to income constraints, it is interesting that the very expression of the desire by better-off children suggests, again, their wider horizons and greater aspirations.

CONCLUSION

To the extent that children pressurise parents, or that parents put pressure on themselves to ensure that their children have access to similar experiences to their peers, it is clear that family budgets are potentially under great strain from the activity choices of children. Children from both socio-economic backgrounds had many activities in common – eg, sport, television, reading, listening to music and socialising with friends. However, there were more options available to the more affluent children and, when younger, their spare time, particularly at weekends, was more structured. In the older age groups, there was a stronger tendency for less affluent boys to be involved in crime; though soft drugs were generally perceived of in a positive light by the young men from both backgrounds. The young women were generally anti-crime.

Children and young adults from both socio-economic backgrounds found the available leisure facilities inadequate and too expensive to use often, if at all. In fact, none of the older children thought that they were well provided for by the community in terms of leisure facilities and this was one reason given by the less affluent children for crime and joyriding.

All children found it difficult to list activities that they wished to do. Moreover, of those that they did identify, few related to those day-to-day activities which would require access to local, inexpensive facilities, the lack of which they bemoaned. It appears that, irrespective of background, children have become resigned to their lot of inadequate and expensive facilities. Television is one easy way of solving the problem of 'what to do', rather than a favourite pastime, and is apparently used in this way by many children, particularly the less affluent. Computers also fulfil this role for many children, mainly boys.

Whilst many of the day-to-day, less expensive things which children do and enjoy were similar, irrespective of their socio-economic background, there are some, more expensive, activities to which children from less affluent backgrounds do not aspire or, indeed, do not even think of doing. It seems that children only find it possible to aspire to extensions of activities which they have already experienced. The stark differences in holiday experiences between the two groups provide the best example of this. More affluent children, who had more, longer holidays, in better accommodation, and who were more likely to have been abroad on holiday, were more likely to want to go travelling abroad. The less affluent children who, if they had a holiday at all, were most likely to rely on holidays or day trips within Britain, simply wanted 'a holiday' per se, rather than wishing to travel the world.

These differences between the activity aspirations of children from different backgrounds are in stark contrast to the common culture of acquisition discussed in Chapter Two. It seems that less affluent children do indeed learn to limit their ambitions to participate in more expensive activities, while actually doing much the same things on a day-to-day basis as their more affluent peers.

NOTES

1. G Murdock, P Hartmann, and P Gray, 'Contextualising home computing – resources and practices' in R Silverstone and E Hirsch (eds), *Consuming Technologies – media and information in domestic space*, Routledge, 1992, p151.
2. *Ibid*, p156.
3. Central Statistical Office, *Social Focus on Children*, HMSO, 1994, p48.
4. *Ibid*, p53.
5. J Eckstein (ed), 'Television and radio; film and culture' in *Cultural Trends*, Vol. 17, Policy Studies Institute, 1993, p36.
6. B Gunter and J L McAleer, *Children and Television: the one-eyed monster?* Routledge, 1990, pp179-180.
7. Cited in G Comstock, *Television and the American Child*, Academic Press Inc, 1991, p84.
8. *Ibid*, p129.
9. Gunter and McAleer, *op cit*, p120.
10. See, for example, A Lareau, *Home Advantage: social class and parental intervention in elementary education*, Falmer, 1989.
11. Central Statistical Office, *Social Trends*, HMSO, 1994.

4 'Keeping up appearances': peer pressure and children's clothes

Karl Ashworth, Robert Walker, Sue Middleton, Karen Kellard, Anne Peaker, Michelle Thomas

INTRODUCTION

Parents firmly believe their children's friends are a major source of financial pressure to have and to do particular things, and Chapters Two and Three have shown the extent to which children have, and want to have, similar things to each other.

The need to fit in with their peers and the fear of being identifiably different emerged strongly and consistently throughout our work with children, as it did with parents. The clothes which children wear are perhaps the most obvious means by which children seek to fit in or, conversely, can be excluded by their peers. In this chapter we describe what children had to say about the extent, nature and result of peer group pressure in relation to clothes.

THE CAUSES AND CONSEQUENCES OF PRESSURE

Children experience pressure from their peers to wear 'acceptable' clothes from an early age. They quickly become aware of the consequences of wearing inappropriate clothing, either through direct experience or through watching other children on the receiving end. The following conversation with the youngest group of less affluent children, who attended a school with a non-uniform policy, reveals some of the things which can happen to a child who is seen as not dressing appropriately.

Interviewer	'Why is it important to look good then?'
Jane	'If you look good people think you look like you're dressed up nice and, but if you're dressed up not very nice people go outside, "look at her!", nasty people like that.'
Ben	'If you wear just plain clothes, like you don't wear jackets with them, you just wear plain, they think that you've just got plain clothes and you haven't got no clothes like. So if you wear clean clothes nobody will pick on you and say, "look at that".'
Interviewer	'What do the kids at school say, the nasty kids at school, to people who aren't dressed right?'
Ben	'Sometimes they say, "Look at the horrible clothes that he's got on."'
Jane	'"I'm not playing with you, you look horrible!".'
	LA, M and F, 7 years

These children are clearly aware of the dangers of 'standing out' if they are not well-dressed and of the verbal abuse which is likely to result, as well as the possibility of social exclusion ('I'm not playing with you') which can accompany the verbal abuse.

The reasons which children gave for these pressures related to the danger of not keeping up with fashion and the stigmatising effects of being seen as too poor to afford acceptable clothes. Indeed, the price of clothes was an issue only for the less affluent children. Their more affluent peers were solely concerned with fashion.

Interviewer	'Do you think it's important to be in fashion?'
Jenny	'Well, yes. You might get picked on or something like that and you feel really embarrassed ... Like at school, people make fun of like, if you haven't got baggy enough jeans, people go, "Oh look, they're skin-tight jeans", or something like that.'
	MA, F, 11 years

Interviewer	'What would make somebody an odd one out?'
Kate	'If like, they hadn't kept up with the fashion or something.'
Laura	'Perhaps when they've got to wear shoes and they come in right cheap trainers.'
Kate	'Someone could come in right dear Adidas trainers and someone come in right cheap trainers.'
Interviewer	'What would happen?'
Laura	'They'd get beat up.'
	LA, F, 7 years

It seems that, while children from both socio-economic backgrounds have fashion-based pressures exerted on them, less affluent children are more aware of the financial implications of keeping up appearances.

These pressures appear to increase at secondary school, particularly for the younger teenagers. The girls below from the more affluent school were talking about their 'non-uniform' day, when they are allowed to 'parade' out of uniform:

Lucy	'Everybody's going to wear stuff that's "in", trendy, and, like you've got to come in something that's really big and baggy.'
Interviewer	'So what happens to people who don't have the right clothes and don't keep up with the fashion?'
Fiona	'People probably go around teasing them.'
	MA, F, 13 years

Girls of the same age from the less affluent school, which did not have a uniform policy, described much the same situation. When asked about the effect of not having 'designer labels,' one girl said:

Mandy	'They hassle you. They just say nasty things like, "you get your shoes from the tip", and stuff like that.'
	LA, F, 13 years

While peer pressure to conform to clothing norms still existed at age 16 years, by this time young people believed they were more resistant to pressure. They felt they had more individual choice over which fashion to follow than when they were younger. The following group of girls described the pressure to wear designer labels which they had experienced when younger.

Carol	'If somebody had something on that was – say everybody had a Naf Naf jumper you'd feel different because you hadn't got one.'
Sharon	'You'd feel left out.'
Denise	'It's like the trend ain't it. Like fashion and that. Just because everyone's got one then you think, oh, you've got to have one.'
Amy	'Yes, it's not necessary that you're going to like it, but they've got it on, so you want one.'
	LA, F, 16 years

Similarly, when asked what happens to young people who do not wear clothes with the right labels, older girls were less willing to give in to the pressure:

Lauren	'It's just verbal abuse really. I wouldn't say there was really big fist fights but...'
Interviewer	'Do you think that puts a lot of pressure on you to buy the right clothes or doesn't it bother you?'
Emma	'Well, it shouldn't bother you really but...'
Sophie	'It don't really bother me.'
Claire	'It does in a way I suppose but...'
Sophie	'I just buy what I wanna buy, I don't care what anybody else thinks.'
	MA, F, 16 years

It seems that younger children in particular from both socio-economic backgrounds are pressured by their peers to wear particular types of clothing. Although this pressure usually takes the form of verbal abuse, taunts and name-calling, it can also sometimes result in physical abuse. Less affluent children are likely to be stigmatised both on grounds of their poverty and their failure to conform to the latest fashions.

CHILDREN'S RESPONSES TO PRESSURE

It would not be surprising if children, witnessing the dire consequences of wearing unacceptable clothing, unanimously responded by demanding new clothes as soon as each new fashion trend emerged. However, the children often showed a surprising degree of ambivalence towards fashion in general and designer labels in particular. It did not appear to be the case that all of the more affluent children received fashionable clothes whilst their less affluent counterparts did not. Boys and girls from both socio-economic groups had some fashionable, or brand-named clothes, but often also had a selection of mundane clothing. Their attitudes to brand names and fashion were similarly mixed, some saying that brand names did not matter, others disagreed.

Interviewer	'They've got to be named?'
Lynne	'Not really. I've got some [jeans] upstairs in my bedroom – not a fashion name.'
Interviewer	'It doesn't have to be a fashion name then?'
Lynne	'Not necessarily – just as long as they're good quality.'
	LA, F, 11 years
Interviewer	'Do you ever choose anything because of the label, because of the name?'

Sean	'Sometimes. Not all of my clothes have got labels on.'
Oliver	'If it's got a design on it you've got to like the design.'
Scott	'Yes, you've got to like the design to like the T-shirt.'
Oliver	'Anyway, you can't always have a name on them because they get really expensive.'
	MA, M, 11 years

However, children have a range of justifications, apart from peer-group pressure, for wanting brand-name clothes, the most common of which are quality and comfort.

Lee	'Yeah cause for Christmas I want some Levi jeans ... Yeah 'cause I just like wearing them 'cause they last a right long time. But the problem is for my age they are about £40 to get some jeans. Yeah, I'll have to put some pocket money into them. Like, my Mum and Dad will go, "£40 for some jeans!" but I'll still want them just because they're comfortable and everybody wears Levis and that.'
	MA, M, 13 years

Others were less impressed by designer labels and some of the girls, in particular, had a sophisticated view of brand names.

Charlotte	'The thing is, new trends come in every day, so like, you get one thing and then you want another that's just come in.'
Marilyn	'Like, Coasters, you know, like those really expensive trainers – about £100, well, my uncle says, "you're not paying for the trainers, you're paying for the name".'
Interviewer	'Do you agree with that?'
Marilyn	'Well, no, not really.'
Interviewer	'What about clothes with designer labels?'
Marilyn	'I just get the ones I like, I'm not bothered about the name.'
Steph	'Who's going to see a label anyway.'
Charlotte	'I think a lot of people say you're paying for the name, which you are, but if you pay for something by Reebok you know that they've got good quality. If you buy something with no name, when it comes to trainers, you think, like, whether to trust them or not because they've got no name on them.'
	MA, F, 13 years

This ambivalence towards the need to have brand names contrasts with the pressures described earlier. It seems that children, while acknowledging the existence of pressure, are unwilling to admit to giving in to it. They prefer to see themselves as in control and resistant to pressure, particularly as they get older.

It may be that realisation of the expense and, hence, impossibility of keeping up with new and rapidly changing fashions quells the fear of the consequences of not doing so. Evidence of this was found among the 16-year-olds with whom we talked. By this age, young women in particular are taking responsibility for shopping for their own clothes, often paying for, or at least contributing towards, the item. Their resulting financial awareness limits their aspirations for fashion and brand names.

Interviewer	'Does it matter what label it's got on?'
Marion	'No.'
Diana	'I think everybody goes through a stage where they want to wear designer clothes though, don't they?'
Marion	'Because it's like the trend, isn't it?'
Diana	'Yes, I have done.'
Marion	'But it doesn't bother me any more.'
Jackie	'When you grow up you don't worry about it any more.'
Interviewer	'So it's something you go through when you're younger?'
Diana	'Because like now, I buy most of my own clothes and you realise that you can't afford to buy everything that you want, everything with designer names on.'
	LA, F, 16 years

While designer names were less of an issue at this age, clothes were still often chosen with the reaction of peers in mind.

Anne	'I suppose everyone will go [ice-skating] in jeans or leggings and it'll not really matter because you're actually not going out where loads of people will see you. I think that's the only time when really everybody gets dressed-up ... You always get more dressed-up, don't you, and look better because there's people who you're mixing with who'd have better clothes, so you've got to look better – to like not fit in; but not stand out either.'
	MA, F, 16 years

It is clear that the pressure to be in fashion and to wear brand-named clothes is particularly strong among younger children from all socio-economic groups. This is confirmed by parents who believe their children to be more or less totally at the mercy of the latest peer-defined fashion craze, particularly at school (see Chapter Five). Our work with parents also suggests that the resistance to fashion shown by older children is a product of their experience of parental unwillingness or inability to pay the cost of keeping up with new fashions.

SECOND-HAND CLOTHES AND 'HAND-ONS'

Second-hand clothes and those received from other members of the family ('hand-ons') can help alleviate the considerable expense of children's clothing (see Chapter Nine), always assuming that children can be persuaded to wear them!

Most junior school children from both areas commonly received hand-ons from family members and friends of the family. Second-hand clothes, bought from jumble sales or other outlets, were mentioned only by children in the less affluent primary school who disliked both hand-ons and second-hand clothes:

Interviewer	'What's wrong with second-hand clothes?'
Jason	'They're too old. Old and dirty and [brother] used to wear them.'
	LA, M, 7 years

Interviewer	'Do you ever get given clothes that you don't like?'
Lisa	'Yes. I never wear them. I'd probably put them in my wardrobe.'
Karen	'I'd get a pair of scissors and rip them up.'
Graham	'I put them in the back of my drawer and wait until my Dad gets them out.'
	LA, M & F, 7 years

All the children in the following group got hand-ons, but no one liked wearing them.

Michelle	'Yeah! But I don't wear them though.'
Interviewer	'Why not?'
Michelle	'Don't like to wear other people's clothes.'
Louise	'No. Every time they give 'em me I just shove 'em in dustbin.'
Interviewer	'Why?'
Louise	'They either give me clothes that are too big or too short.'
Interviewer	'But why wouldn't you wear second-hand clothes?'
Louise	'I wouldn't dare. They'd call you scrubby.'
	LA, M & F, 7 years

The fear of peer rejection can again be seen. Children will only wear second-hand clothes under protest, because of their association with poverty. When they are forced to wear them they suffer as a result.

In contrast, the more affluent younger children, who received hand-ons but not second-hand clothes, seemed not only to accept wearing them, but also liked them. It may be that hand-ons play a different role in the wardrobe of affluent children, being additional to a large stock of new clothes. For less affluent children, by contrast, hand-ons are more likely to substitute for new clothes.

In general, the secondary school children did not get second-hand clothes or hand-ons and, although some of the older girls mentioned that they might buy second-hand if they were in fashion, the idea of such clothes was not popular.

Interviewer	'Do you think it makes any difference that the clothes are second-hand and not new?
Veronica	'No.'
Marie	'You don't feel as nice. You don't feel as good, like, even if you like it you don't feel as good as if it were new.
Barbara	'If it were only your sister's or whatever it doesn't really matter, because they're like part of you aren't they.'
	MA, F, 13 years
Interviewer	'Would you ever wear second-hand clothes?'
Lois	'Yes. If it looked all right.'
Debbie	'It depends. I'm right funny on stuff like that. I don't know. I don't know where it's been, so. I don't know I'm just funny like that.'
Interviewer	'With second-hand clothes, is there anything you wouldn't have?'
Felicity	'I don't think I'd buy a stretch top because it's too close to the body, and I wouldn't wear underwear.'
	MA, F, 16 years

These girls are reflecting the views expressed by parents (see Chapter Nine), that second-hand clothes such as jumpers, T-shirts and jeans are more acceptable than those which have been in close contact with the body. Therefore, used clothing was more acceptable when it came from family members than from strangers.

CONCLUSION

Children use clothes as a basis for making judgements about others. Some of these inferences relate to poverty and the stigma attached to it; others relate to notions of 'fashion'. Children are aware from an early age of the need to 'conform' to the clothing expectations of their peers. Knowledge of the consequences of failure to conform – social exclusion and taunting – can lead to feelings of embarrassment and isolation, and such pressures can weigh heavily on the shoulders of some, particularly younger, children. Although by the age of 16, children seem better able to cope with, and are more resistant to, such pressures, this is of little consolation to less affluent parents struggling to meet the clothing demands of younger children.

The fears of poorer parents that their children may be stigmatised for looking poor, as well as for not keeping up with fashion, seem to be borne out. The consequences for children in terms of physical, as well as verbal, abuse can indeed be severe.

Melissa	'I feel sorry for Lorraine.'
Janet	'Just because she's got a pair of trainers called "Pony". Sometimes she gets beat up.'
	LA, F, 13 years

5 'Whatever happened to free education?': the cost of school

Sue Middleton and Michelle Thomas

INTRODUCTION

Education, along with health care, is one of the few areas of life where a family's economic circumstances might be thought irrelevant to a child's life chances and experiences in 1990s Britain. Britain has a state education system which provides free compulsory education for all children between the ages of five and sixteen. Throughout the massive educational upheavals of the 1980s and 1990s the concept of free state education, paid for from general taxation, has remained fundamentally unchallenged. Whilst parents have retained the option to purchase private education for their children if they so wish, and if they can afford to, for the 95 per cent of parents whose children remain in the state sector, the assumption has been that education comes free.

Parents have a different tale to tell. Throughout our discussions, mothers of school-age children from all socio-economic groups, and living in different parts of the country, continually referred to the additional financial pressures which school now brings to the family budget. Although parents reported requests for financial contributions to all aspects of their child's school life, we have chosen to concentrate in this chapter on those areas which were identified as being mainly responsible for financial demands. We explore parents' understanding of the reasons for such demands and show how they experience them as a series of pressures from different sources within the school. Their reactions to these pressures are mediated through a combination of parental aspirations, guilt, economic circumstances and, above all, the determination to ensure that their child is not excluded or made to feel 'different' – the right to 'participation' with which this book is centrally concerned. As Chapter Seven shows, children are only too well aware of the persuasiveness of the 'I've got to have it for school' argument!

WHAT PARENTS PAY FOR

Interviewer	'Do you often get requests from school for money?'
•	'Oh, yeah.'
•	'All the time.'
•	'If it's not one thing it's another.'
•	'Yeah, every little thing costs money.'
•	'Letters saying money for this, money for that.'
•	'We get a letter nearly every other day.'
•	'And if you don't want to make voluntary contributions…'
•	'Oh yeah, that's right.'
•	'And if they make anything they've got to pay for it.'
•	'They make it awkward if you don't give.'
•	'Yeah.'

6 – 10 year olds

The strength of reaction of this group of mothers, who were discussing the needs of a child aged between six and ten years old, was typical and was not confined to this age group. Indeed, parents described requests for financial contributions covering all aspects of school life from skiing holidays, to money to pay for items made in woodwork and electronics classes.

Frances (1)   'Well, I got a letter they brought home yesterday [about a skiing trip], £496, plus you've got your insurance.'
11 – 16 years

Sally (2)   'Ours do woodwork, 'cause Z's just made a carousel. And they had to pay £1 before they could bring it home.'
6 – 10 years

The amounts of money being requested also vary widely, from £800 for an educational cruise to Egypt, to 25 pence a year towards the cost of cookery.

However, within this overall context of continual demands for money, three areas of school life emerged as being of particular concern to parents: school trips and holidays; GCSEs; and school uniform.

SCHOOL TRIPS AND HOLIDAYS

Legislation now prevents schools from 'charging' parents for school trips. Parents can legally be asked to make a voluntary contribution only towards the cost of the trip. While some of the, usually better-off, parents were aware of this, the majority were not, and were equally uncertain about the effect of not paying the 'voluntary contribution'.

Linda (1)	'You don't have to pay.'
Jane (3)	'It's a voluntary contribution.'
Leslie	'It's supposed to be a voluntary contribution.'
Jenny (3)	'But unless you're on income support you can't go, yeah...'
Leslie	'Yeah, but if you really can't you don't have to.'
Kate (2)	'But does your child still go?'
Leslie	'Yes.'
Karen	'Does it? I didn't know...'
Leslie	'They can't exclude them.'
Sandra (2)	'But the problem is, if not enough parents pay...'
Leslie	'Yeah, they've got to cover it.'

6 – 10 years

Schools get round the 'voluntary' nature of the contribution by pointing out to parents that unless sufficient 'voluntary contributions' are received, the trip will not take place. Parents resent this pressure, regarding it as a form of coercion which is difficult to resist.

Joyce (1)	'You see, you get letters saying okay there's a trip going, all contributions are voluntary, but if you don't pay...'
Chris (2)	'...the trip can't go ahead.'
Joyce	'...the trip can't go ahead so you feel ... that if you don't pay for your child that trip can't go ahead for the other children so you feel guilty.'

11 – 16 years

Sue (3)	'But if there's not enough contributions, nobody would be allowed to go, so if you don't pay you feel guilty in case not enough people pay, and the trip is cancelled ... I've got three at school now, so if they all go on a trip, it'll be like a quid each, which doesn't sound much, but £3 it's a lot more.'

6 – 16 years

Most schools apparently include in their requests for payment an indication that financial help is available for those who are on low incomes and/or income support (IS). Others offer arrangements for weekly payments which parents on low incomes appreciate as a method of spreading the cost. However, such offers of financial help are often worded in a discouraging fashion and, in any event, those parents who might have been eligible are unwilling to ask for reasons of pride.

Leslie (3)   'Well, I am actually on income support so if I want to, but I never have, I can go to the school and say, "Look, I can't afford to pay for this, can it come out of the school funds". I never have … because what if they turn round and say no.'

Anna (3)   'They don't word it welcoming you coming in to ask.'

1 – 16 years

The number and range of requests which parents reported for such 'voluntary contributions' for school trips and holidays were enormous and can start at a very young age. Parents with children as young as five years old reported being asked for £5 for a trip to the pantomime, although such requests were relatively rare for this age group. It seems that the financial pressure is limited until the child reaches secondary school, at which point parents begin to discriminate clearly between 'holidays' – those trips which are seen as simply for pleasure, and 'field trips' – which are related to the school curriculum.

Lorraine (3)   'If it's really, really important and to do with their school work. If it's just a trip for leisure … It depends on the trip. If they really do need it for the school and everybody's going then they ought to go.'

0 – 5 years

Parental resentment focuses on the requests for leisure trips and holidays which parents view as too frequent, too expensive, and, in some cases, too dangerous. The parents see school trips as an excuse for teachers to go away with their spouses and have a good time subsidised by parents.

Pat (2)   'Now the teacher, the same teacher, took them to Belgium the year before and his wife went. I think they are just in it for a free holiday, if they can arrange one…'

Carol (1)   'They do, I know it from that perspective, we've got friends who are teachers and it's, "Take the wife…".'

11 – 16 years

However, some parents did see a positive side to these holidays, particularly the role which they play in making children more independent. Perhaps unsurprisingly, it was the better-off parents who tended to identify these advantages and justify the expenditure on these grounds. Parents on lower incomes were more likely to castigate the trips as a waste of money. Rather than say that they could not afford them, they justified their refusal to let their children participate on the grounds that turning down such requests was in itself a valuable learning experience for the child.

Emma (1)   'I think that they have to have the opportunity to be away. I'm not talking necessarily about expensive trips, but away from the parents and test themselves and share the friendship ... funnily enough I think that if you are with them they behave differently to when they are somewhere else, they have got more responsibility for themselves and they act differently...'
11 – 16 years

Anna (3)   'I would say if you could afford it ... without going over the top and spoiling them rotten then yes. I think it depends on your circumstances ... that way the child is getting every single thing it wants and no child gets everything otherwise you just grow up selfish...'
11 – 16 years

Some parents went as far as to suggest that schools should not offer such holidays because of the inevitable discriminatory effect on parents on a low income.

Denise (3)   'It sections people out, doesn't it? It does section people out – holidays at school – I think it does. Because it's a shame for parents that can't afford to send their children. Even though the children would love to go.'
11 – 16 years

This is not to say that parents view the requests for funding even for curriculum-related field trips with complete equanimity. There is resentment that they are being asked to pay for things which, if they are part of the curriculum, should be paid for by the school or the local education authority.

Marilyn (3)   'I mean even museums, when they go to a museum, say they are doing a particular piece of work and they go to a particular museum … to see say dinosaurs, the parents are asked would your child like to go and we have to pay. But when you think of something like that perhaps it could be paid for by the education authority.'

11 – 16 years

However, for most parents any trip which is seen to be part of the school curriculum has to be paid for, whatever the cost. A combination of guilt, aspirations for the child and a determination that the child shall not be singled out leads parents to make enormous sacrifices.

Roz (1)   'The fact is we want our children to grow up culturally aware, I don't grudge my child to go to the theatre, it just costs, we don't want to draw them away from these things. I would like them to have the opportunity.'

11 – 16 years

Julie (1)   'Is that trip about £3 or £4 or something? It's not over-expensive, but, like you say, if you've got more than one, it starts to build up. But if you don't give permission for whatever reason, your child stands out. You might as well put a green hat on and stand in the corner.'

6 – 10 years

Jenny (3)   'The thing is people do pay it, don't they? I know somebody last year that was on income support … and she told her ex-husband that if he didn't pay for half of it, he won't be able to see his own son. And I thought that was blackmail, that was awful.'

Karen (3)   'But again, that's pressure isn't it? It's the pressure that parents come under.'

6 – 10 years

This pressure becomes particularly intense as children approach GCSEs, when schools convince parents that trips are not just helpful to the child's education, but an essential part of the GCSE course.

Mandy (2)   'I think you find that the extras do come in as they get into the GCSE course work. There are an awful lot of field trips, theatre to do with the English if they are doing – well, everyone has to do English. There's a lot of those and they are not optional.'

11 – 16 years

While resenting such demands, parents feel that they are left with no choice but to pay, given that the alternative, as they see it, is that the child will be excluded from the examination.

Joyce (1)   'It's probably like one James brought home today. He's got to go to the Potteries for his design and that is compulsory ... and I suppose that is a field trip ... I mean he's got to go but he's got to pay for it.'

Interviewer   'How do you feel about that, he's got to go and you've got to pay for it?'

Joyce   'Well, I'm fortunate obviously, I can afford to do it, but that's not the point.'

Anna (3)   'I don't think you ought to if it's compulsory within the exam...'

Some   'No.'

Anna   'If you want extra tutoring or extra this, that and the other you pay, but if it's got to be, I don't think you ought to 'cause they have set that curriculum for every child.'

                11 – 16 years

However, the financial demands of GCSE courses extend far beyond the cost of school trips and it is to this that we now turn.

THE COSTS OF GCSEs

As a child approaches GCSEs parents report increasing financial pressures, not just from school but at home as well. The need for children to have the best possible facilities to do homework in peace can cause family conflict. Costs associated with computers, furniture and trying to ensure that the child has her/his own room can also result in pressure.

Rona (3)   'I had my house repossessed so we were very fortunate to get a brand new three-bedroomed house. So out of bad came some good. They did end up with a room of their own and at their age I thought it was vital anyway, when we moved they were both in exams.'

                11 – 16 years

Some parents go to great lengths to provide a good working environment for their child – whether s/he wants it or not!

Carol (2)   'My Mam bought my brother a fantastic table and chair to do his homework on and he never used it ... I think a lot of it is if you've bought it for them to do their homework ... And that's the problem, because you've bought it for that reason, and they'll see you in hell first before they use it...'

Leslie (3)   'What we should say is I bought you this to stand some flowers on and you can use it for your homework if you really want to.'

11 – 16 years

However, it is the pressure for children to have computers at home for their GCSE work which parents seem to be feeling most acutely and ambivalently. Although schools are not saying to parents that it is essential that their child has a computer at home, parents themselves are drawing their own conclusions as a result of practical experience.

Jo (2)   'We were shown all the projects on computer as an example of what was expected of James this year. And when we said, "We haven't got anything that would do that", and they said "Well you haven't got to", but as you can see...'

Josie (1)   'You get better marks.'

Jo   '...it makes a much better result and therefore the marker is going to look a bit more favourably on it. So I am tempted to say it is essential. If you are talking about for GCSEs...'

11 – 16 years

Parents on low incomes feel these pressures acutely.

Kathie (3)   'It's difficult ... mine haven't got one, we haven't got one. Our financial circumstances – I've tried looking for a second-hand one, and you just can't get them to the standard that my daughter needs, the eldest is doing computer studies ... Nowadays ... they use them such a lot and in their projects, their work is presented in computer format, much neater than hand-written. Well, yes, I would like my children to have one, but I can't afford it. But it's getting to the stage where it's becoming, I think, essential. You should look at the projects when you go round the colleges now. They are all done on computer.'

11 – 16 years

GCSE courses bring other, more direct, financial demands from schools. Parents reported being asked to pay for a range of items connected with these courses. Schools insist on GCSE course work being presented in ring binders and on a range of specialist equipment for particular subjects: art and design; physical education (PE); and even books for English.

Carol (1)   'We have to pay at school for books that they can annotate for their exams. So we are given the option of them having their own books but we have to pay for them because otherwise they have to share. And obviously if you are doing an exam you want to annotate, when the teacher's going through a passage you want to annotate it, well you can't annotate a school book can you?'
          11 – 16 years

Parents feel they have no choice but to pay up, given their aspirations for their children. They feel that schools are aware of this and are putting unfair pressure on them.

Marilyn (3)   '...maybe they should think about paying for it as well because they're opting out, the Government is opting out because the parents are not going to say no.'
          11 – 16 years

The parents felt that the schools did not warn them of the likely financial demands of particular GCSE courses, which then came as a nasty shock.

Leslie (3)   'The other thing I think is if they know these things are going to crop up during the course, it's course work, they ought to send out information on the course that the child is going to take and how much it is going to cost so that you know and then you can budget for it. I mean if that comes up all of a sudden...'

Joyce (1)   'Which it has, James just asked today if he could pay £6, I've got to go on this course.'

Anna (3)   'Yeah, 'cause we had the letters, was it the other week, what exams they wanted to take. Now that's just saying, as you say, just exams you want, it's not saying how much extra each one will cost you. So you put down your nine lessons she wants to take, then all of a sudden through the next two or three years it's "Can I have this, can I have that...?"'
          11 – 16 years

GCSE costs do not, of course, arise until the child is 14 years old. However, at an earlier stage in the child's education, schools make other financial demands which parents find equally difficult to avoid or resist.

SCHOOL UNIFORM

The parents to whom we listened supported school uniform in principle. They greeted its imposition with relief, at whatever age the schools demanded it. Mothers from the north of England described the two advantages of school uniform from the parents' perspective: it stops arguments and helps to relieve peer group pressure and competition:

Eve (1)	'It's easier to get them dressed as well.'
Alison (2)	'No arguments in the morning about what they're wearing. It's uniform and that's it.'
Karen (3)	'And they all look the same. There's no competition. It's brilliant.'
Interviewer	'Does anybody disagree with that?'
Diane (3)	'No, it's brilliant.'
Chorus	'No.'

11 – 16 years

Most primary school children did not have to wear a uniform, much to parents' regret. In contrast, most of the secondary schools did have a uniform, even if this was only a requirement to wear particular colours.

However, the high level of support for the principle of school uniform is being undermined by the way in which some schools implement it. In particular, parents complained about schools which insist that children wear clothes displaying the school badge. These clothes, which many parents reported to be of poor quality, can only be bought from the school and sew-on badges are not made available. Presumably schools are using this method to raise funds, a fact of which parents are aware but unsympathetic.

Alice (1)	'When he first started I were paying on average £4 or £5 per polo shirt but now they are saying that if they take their sweatshirt off they've got to display the badge and the polo shirts are now £10.50...'
Joanne (1)	'Why can't you just have a sew-on badge?'
Felicity (3)	'Because they're not making the money.'
Caroline (1)	'It's their way of making a profit, they've got the monopoly...'

Joanne (1)   'It's disgusting that.'
                   11 – 16 years

Leslie (3)   'I mean at … school if you really want to you can pay £9.50,
                   or at least you did when my daughter started, and have them
                   wearing a black sweatshirt with a big yellow band across it to
                   show their house, if you really wanted to, and it was very
                   badly put together and extremely expensive.'
                   11 – 16 years

School demands for the provision of standard PE kit also came in for
criticism, in particular requests for expensive specialist footwear, such
as football boots and hockey boots, which might only be worn for a
few weeks during the season. These criticisms were compounded by
the uncertainty which parents felt about the extent to which schools
are legally entitled to enforce either uniform in general or PE kit in
particular.

Mandy (2)   'Well I actually have an ongoing thing with the school because
                   my youngest … they insisted she had to have hockey boots.
                   Now I said, "We have five children that we are responsible
                   for between us, four of them are in full-time education, it's
                   not as if she's going to do hockey for the whole year", could
                   they tell me whether it was a statutory requirement for a
                   child to have hockey boots … but the teachers couldn't tell
                   me…'
                   11 – 16 years

Julie (1)   'In our school it's compulsory you see, so you don't have a
                   choice…'
Sandy (2)   'Then they've got to wear it. I think all children should wear
                   it.'
Anne (2)   'Well, I thought the schools weren't allowed to say you got
                   to wear them.'
Sandy (2)   'A lot of schools do though.'
Anne (2)   'I know they do but they are not allowed to. If you turn up
                   and you've not bought one they either give your child what
                   they've got at school or they leave your child alone, they're
                   not allowed to say you've got to have a uniform.'
                   6 – 10 years

Whatever the school's policy on school uniform, the pressure on
many parents is unrelieved. The strictest uniform policy still leaves

scope for fashion trends and the resulting peer group pressure can be intense.

Christine (2)	'Even if they've got a school uniform, it'll be the bag that they are carrying.'
Chorus	'Yes, that's true.'
Joanne (1)	'Mine's got Puma bags.'
Christine (2)	'My son just had a plain black bag when he first started his school, a plain black bag and he was not picked on but he weren't comfortable because it hadn't got a name on, this bag, and he wouldn't have it so he ended up putting some of his own money towards one that had got a name on.'
	11 – 16 years

This need for children to 'fit in' again ran throughout our discussions of school uniform. Parents were emphatic that every child should have the right to any item of uniform insisted upon by the school as an essential minimum and made allowance for this in their budget standard. After all, this was the area where children could be most easily 'singled out' if they were not wearing the correct clothes.

Interviewer	'...you seem to be saying that it's essential the child can have it?'
Janet (2)	'Yeah, because they'll look different from the other kids.'
Chorus	'They've got to have it.'
Avril (2)	'There's enough things you can think about at school to get picked on without looking different.'
	2 – 5 years

Some schools are obviously aware of the financial demands which school uniform can make on family budgets and make provision for parents to have access to second-hand uniform items. However, as we have shown in Chapter Four, children are often unwilling to accept second-hand clothing, fearing the reaction of their peers. The financial pressure on many, less well-off, parents remains intense, particularly as school uniform is not usually defined as an essential item under the social fund.

Anita (3)	'I tell you, school uniform, when David started at ... this term, I had to buy a school uniform. I got two weeks' income support because it was a bank holiday and I had to buy a school uniform out of my income support. I tried to get a loan from the DSS, but they told me that I couldn't

have one, because I couldn't afford to pay it back, so I ended up having to buy the school uniform out of my income support, so the following week was very lean.'

6 – 16 years

School uniform is a mixed blessing. It can reduce the overall cost of clothing a child, restrict arguments about week-day dress and remove at least some of the competitive pressure among children for the latest designer label goods. However, schools which operate as a monopoly supplier of uniform items, or impose a rigid uniform policy which includes expensive but rarely used items, continue to put parents under financial pressures which they resent. Children still find ways of setting fashion trends within the overall uniform policy. This combination of school and peer group pressure is impossible for parents to resist. Their child must not be seen to be different.

CONCLUSION

The notion that state education in Britain is, or ever was, totally free is probably a myth. School uniform has always had to be provided, and schools have always had their outings and visits. However, it seems that the current level and range of school-related financial demands had many of the parents to whom we listened at their wits' end. They do everything in their power to meet these demands in order to ensure that their child is not 'picked on' and to allow the child to have every opportunity of succeeding educationally. Parents have little awareness of the background of recent legislative change which has caused financial problems for many schools. The almost daily requests for money, which are a manifestation of the new financial world in which schools are forced to operate, are seen by parents as unfair pressure on their own, often limited, budgets. They believe that schools are taking advantage of their inability to say 'no' when it is their child's education which is at stake. As one mother said,

Mandy (2)   '...it's a war of attrition isn't it between you, the kids, the school, trying to balance all the demands.'

11 – 16 years

6 'Just something to laugh about': children and advertising

Karen Kellard, Robert Walker, Karl Ashworth, Sue Middleton, Anne Peaker and Michelle Thomas

INTRODUCTION

The previous two chapters have examined the financial pressures on parents, from children's peers and from their schools. This chapter explores the effect of advertising on children, and considers the pressure that advertisers can exert on parents by way of children.

Advertisers and some researchers would argue that advertising plays a vital role in economic and cultural socialisation and, indeed, buying and selling are a fundamental part of Western culture.[1] Others argue that advertising to children creates materialism, is misleading and can lead to parent–child conflict.

Whichever viewpoint is taken, it is indisputable that advertising is difficult to avoid. In relation to television advertising, 99 per cent of households with children have access to at least one television set,[2] with at least two channels showing commercials, and many households also have access to satellite stations. Children in the United States are, on average, exposed to some 20,000 commercial messages each year, and while Britain is some way behind, it is not in an entirely different league.[3] In recent years, TV commercials have become more complex and creative. New concepts have been developed, such as advertisements that run as a mini-series, some that are more like pop videos and others that seem to bear no relevance to the product at all.

Television advertising is a favourite medium for targeting children.[4] Advertisers want their commercials to be seen and remembered by children, to induce them to spend their own money and to persuade their parents to make a purchase.

This chapter explores how children respond to advertising. It describes children's awareness and understanding of advertising and those advertisements which they remember and those to which they respond.

AWARENESS OF ADVERTISING

By the age of four, most children are believed to have the ability to distinguish between an advertisement and a programme.[5]

Our research suggests that different forms of advertising become salient at different ages. At age seven and eight some children were a little unclear about forms of advertising other than TV commercials. Some even included 'road signs' and 'pelican crossings' in their descriptions of advertising, but all recognised the function of television advertising. In contrast, the 10- to 11-year-olds recalled many different types of advertising including: on hoardings; at the cinema; in magazines and catalogues; on the sides of vans; and posters displayed in the windows of empty shops.

Interviewer	'Where else do you see adverts?'
Anthony	'On posters and things in town.'
Interviewer	'Do you notice those?'
Justin	'It's because they're big. You can't miss them, they stand out.'
Anthony	'They're normally about banks and accounts and things.'

MA, M, 10 – 11 years

Boys of this age and younger frequently cited computer magazines:

Dean	'The back of the cover shows you the graphics … It shows you on the comic what the latest games are.'

MA, M, 7 – 8 years

By 15 to 16 years old, young people seemed more restrictive in their recall, mentioning only television and, occasionally, radio advertising.

Mail-order catalogues as a form of advertising were mentioned more frequently by children from less affluent areas. This may be because less affluent families are more likely to use catalogue shopping as a way of spreading the cost whereby they

- 'give people money when they come each week.'

LA, M, 7 – 8 years

Although children were aware of different forms of advertising, discussions always centred around TV commercials. This may be because they found TV commercials exciting and, for the younger children, easier to understand than other advertising media.

Jane   'I think reading adverts is really boring, I like watching adverts.'
Katharine   'Yes, watching adverts is better because you don't have to do
              anything.'
                        MA, F, 11 – 12 years

The children's interest in advertising was obvious from the lively discussions which took place. Most of the children liked television commercials in particular and saw them as a natural part of our society.

RECALL OF ADVERTISEMENTS

Children's recall of advertisements was extensive at all ages, although boys and girls seemed to recall different advertisements at different ages.

Younger children tended to remember the commercial itself (often in some detail) rather than the product or brand name:

Ross   'I like this advert where this lady's writing a letter and there's
              green slime dropping down her leg and this big tail comes
              out and gets her … and then she says "come and have a cup
              of tea" and then…'
Interviewer   'What's it advertising, do you know?'
Ross   'No.'
                        LA, GU, 7 – 8 years

The exception was for advertisements for a product that they already owned or had a desire to own, especially toys, such as Sylvanian families (girls), CupCakes (girls), and computer games (mostly boys).

Chloe   'I like the advertisement for the Sylvanian families … they've
              got all the cakes.'
Interviewer   'Do you collect Sylvanian families?'
Chloe   'No.'
Interviewer   'Would you like to?'
Chloe   'Yes.'
                        MA, F, 7 – 8 years

Marcus   'Computers … Sega and Nintendo.'
Interviewer   'Why do you like the computer adverts?'

Dean   'They're all games to buy and decide ... Olympic Games for Sega, Sonic...'

            MA, M, 7 – 8 years

Advertisements for computer systems and computer games were recalled in almost all of the groups, except those involving 15- and 16-year-olds, who had either missed out on the computer-based revolution in home entertainment or lost interest in it.

Indeed, very few children in this age group highlighted particular favourites and the discussions that took place with the oldest children concentrated on advertising in general, or advertisements which they particularly disliked or objected to. They were much less likely to admit to having a 'favourite', unless it was for a product that related more to them as an individual or as a member of a peer group.

Steve   'The Pepsi Max adverts.'

Tim   'Yeah, been there, done it, all that business.'

Steve   'Yeah.'

Lee   'Best advert on telly.'

Robbie   'Sticks in your brain don't it.'

Interviewer '...you said the best advert on telly, why?'

Lee   'I think it's funny ... the Adrenaline boys ... I don't drink any though, I like Coke.'

Tim   'I just watch the advert, it's good, and saying God I wish I was doing that now.'

            MA, M, 15 – 16 years

The 10- and 11-year-olds expressed most interest in advertising and exhibited most knowledge of specific commercials. They recalled adverts for products ranging from food and drinks, to cat food, washing powders, cameras and cigars.

One group of 10- and 11-year-old girls in a school located in an affluent area was particularly interested in advertising and had discussed it in informal groups:

Lisa   'We were talking about them on our table ... yesterday.'

Interviewer 'Why?'

Lisa   'Just something to laugh about, because we like adverts, we imitate adverts.'

            MA, F, 10 – 11 years

The same group of girls in another discussion gave a virtually word-perfect impromptu re-enactment of the Philadelphia cheese commercial (a popular favourite):

Jane   'I like the Philadelphia advert, it's really funny … shall we do
                an impression of it? I'll be the lady with the weird voice, and
                you be the lady at the end of the line, who's phoning.'
                MA, F, 10 – 11 years

Their discussions also filtered into home activities:

Katharine   'We record the adverts, we like giving them marks out of ten
                … we record the adverts and then we watch the adverts
                rather than the programme that we're watching … that's all
                the family and sometimes the friends come round as well …
                she's [member of group] been round once or twice and we
                sit there with our pens and paper marking off the adverts.'
                MA, F, 10 – 11 years

Children differed in how they remembered the advertisements. Younger
children often recalled them because of the jingles or catchphrases.
These were sometimes sung in the playground, often reworded!

Jane   'Dairy cows advert … "we are lucky cows, we live in a
                slaughter house, so we eat our dairy cheese, because we have
                mad cow disease".'
                MA, F, 10 – 11 years

Advertisements did not have to be directed at children to be
remembered. As already noted, children mentioned advertisements
ranging from those for washing powders to cigars:

Katharine   'I used to like the Hamlet adverts but we're not meant to
                watch them, the Hamlet adverts were really brilliant.'
Victoria   'With Russ Abbott on them.'
Katharine   'Yes, he was really good, I like that one where he's in the
                photograph booth and he's sat there and he's trying to comb
                his hair and just as the camera snaps, he goes, and after a few
                minutes, his hair falls down, and he goes like this to put it up
                and the photo takes … and then it goes, Hamlet, the mild
                cigar.'
                MA, F, 10 – 11 years

Different recall at different ages may be due to children's developing
language and communication skills and, in particular, the ability and
willingness to express themselves to the adult researchers. We found
that children from the more affluent areas were more elaborate in
their descriptions of adverts than their less affluent counterparts, who
were often less forthcoming in detail.

THE PURPOSE OF ADVERTISING

It would appear that most children understand the purpose of advertising and are aware of different advertising techniques. Indeed, they were well able, and often did, evaluate what they saw.

In line with earlier research by Greenberg, Fazal and Wober,[6] children of all ages believed that the primary purpose of advertisements was to 'sell something' or to 'make people buy it'. However, some children (particularly in the less affluent areas) emphasised the advertisers' desire to 'to make money' rather than 'to sell the product'. A number even saw advertisements as a desperation measure by the company to 'get rid' of stock:

Nicholas	'I reckon they only put adverts on because they're going out of business.'
Interviewer	'Do you?'
Nicholas	'And they're trying to get more customers back.'
Ryan	'Yeah.'
Interviewer	'Do you? What do others of you think?'
Charlie	'Yeah, they only put it on because … the things which everybody says are crap, they never come on because they always get bought, don't they … like that Daz, they say it's always good and that, but why is it on telly, if it's so good? People would be buying it if it was so good … it just means they ain't getting anything.'
	LA, M, 12 – 13 years

Some of the children had developed cynicism about advertising before their ninth birthday!

Interviewer	'Have you ever wanted something because you saw it advertised on the television?'
Jason	'No… never.'
Interviewer	'Why do you think they advertise if you don't like the things that you see?'
Andrew	'They advertise because they make them look really good in the advert.'
Jason	'Because they want to get money.'
Andrew	'Yes, but they're not that good when you buy them.'
Jason	'I know, sometimes they just break.'
	MA, M, 7 – 8 years

Other children recognised a more positive role for advertising in that it could be a source of knowledge and keep people informed of new products:

Interviewer	'What do you think adverts are for?'
Terri	'It's like, if you want to buy somet' it tells you where you can get it from.'
Ross	'They show you shops like Toys R Us and you can go to Toys R Us and buy what you want.'
	LA, GU, 7 – 8 years

Interviewer	'Why do they make adverts?'
Mark	'To show you what's coming out ... [computer] games, to show you what's coming out.'
	LA, M, 7 – 8 years

By the age of seven and eight, children were very discerning and astute about the objectives of advertisers, if somewhat confused about the operation of credit:

Interviewer	'Why do you think they show all of these advertisements?'
Jamie	'To make money.'
Ashley	'Because they want to get rid of the things.'
Fran	'Like on that advert there's a shop and it's got lots of ... and cutlery in and you can have four years' free credit. Because they want all the furniture shifted because they want to build another one.'
Interviewer	'What does free credit mean?'
Ashley	'Three years' credit.'
Fran	'That means you don't have to pay for three years.'
	LA, GU, 7 – 8 years

In terms of understanding advertising techniques and targeting, even quite young children were generally aware that some commercials were targeted at them, in particular those for sweets, chocolates, computer systems and games machines.

Interviewer	'Do you think any of the adverts are designed for people of your age?'
Charlotte	'Yes, probably the chocolate ones.'
Lisa	'Mega CD.'
Karyn	'Quite a lot of them are, but not like Kwik-Fit or anything like that, or Swithland Motors.'
	MA, F, 10 – 11 years

However, by the age of 11 some children felt that advertising directed at children could be patronising:

Interviewer	'Which do you think might be [aimed at children]?'
Katharine	'...I know, that one about milk, I can't remember the words, but that was supposed to be aimed for teenagers, but that's stupid. But when the older people, they try to make things for teenagers really kind of funky, and...'
Victoria	'They're really babyish.'
Katharine	'It's stupid and we think we've grown up.'

MA, F, 10 – 11 years

Children were also aware that advertisers were competing to sell their products and they drew attention to the commercials that compared one product or brand with another:

Interviewer	'So what sort of things are they trying to say in ... adverts?'
Leanne	'That they are better than the other kinds, like Persil are trying to say that they are better than Ariel Ultra.'
Becky	'But why can't they say things like Daz is better than Ariel or Ariel is better than Daz, is it 'cos they'd get sued?'
Interviewer	'I think it is, yeah ... I think they are not actually allowed to name a...'
Joanne	'But they just do copies of their bottles, just to like show what they mean ... stick a different label on the front.'

MA, F, 12 – 13 years

There was some cynicism about this and other similar techniques, which for this child was based on experience:

Robert	'I buy this magazine every month, about £2.25, and that usually tells you what the latest consoles are coming out an' that, and they have advertising in as well, a lot of advertising, advertising in different magazines but the same company makes them, because I think that's a slight con. 'Cos they've got all these, they make out that one company owns one magazine. Really, they own this magazine, then another one and another one and another one, so it's a bit of a rip off, 'cos they're all competing with each other but they are not really, 'cos they're all getting the same money.'

MA, M, 12 – 13 years

Children also mentioned the technique of repeated advertisements between programmes running as a continuing story:

Anthony	'...you get about three breaks and a bit of the advert on one break and then it carries on in the other.'
Simon	'Yes, Nescafe.'
Justin	'Oh yes, I've seen about all of those.'
Simon	'Same here.'
Interviewer	'Are they good?'
Simon	'No.'
Justin	'I think they are actually.'
Anthony	'Yes, I quite like those ... I like watching them, I'm not bothered about the coffee.'

MA, M, 10 – 11 years

A similar technique in a computer magazine had caught the attention of one child:

Neil	'It's like, there was an advert in one of my computer magazines that said "guess what's coming to your console" and then you had to turn over the page to see, so you suddenly turn over and start reading this advert ... it's a clever one 'cos it like keeps you in suspense and so you flip it over quick and forget about the article you were reading and start reading this thingy. So then you haven't read a lot about it but I think that's a good way to get you...'

MA, M, 12 – 13 years

THE EFFECTS OF ADVERTISING

The fact that children can evaluate advertisements and discriminate between them does not necessarily mean that advertising is ineffectual with children. The discussions revealed many instances where advertising had caused children to buy an item.

Children of all ages – particularly girls – admitted to the effectiveness of food advertising:

Interviewer	'What sort of things would you say work?'
Saskia	'Chocolate and that, like if a new chocolate comes out and I'll say "Oh, I want that, I want to try that".'

LA, F, 10 – 11 years

Interviewer	'Have you ever bought anything through an advertisement ?'
Craig	'Yeah ... what's that new cola, that clear...?'
Roger	'Tab Clear.'

Craig	'Tab Clear … it's like a cola what's see through, like lemonade.'
Thomas	'Like water and it tastes like it as well.'
Craig	'It don't!'
Thomas	'It does!'

LA, M, 10 – 11 years

Television advertising appears to be important in stimulating an awareness of products, especially new ones. Once alerted, some children deliberately try and view the product rather than rely on the advertiser's portrayal:

Phil	'Well, sommut with advertising, you see one thing and it's got this brand new air bubble for new Nikes or something and you think I might as well have a look at them, have a try and put them on and you feel "Oh I like these" and then you buy 'em and it's not from the advert, it's because you tried them on but the adverts like saying these are the trainers you wanna see.'

MA, M, 15 – 16 years

Ryan	'These computer games…'
Christopher	'There's this thingy and it's dragster racing and it goes and it tells you how fast your car goes and I've seen that on telly and I wanted it.'
Ryan	'Computer games, if you see them on telly and they look good then you buy them.'
Interviewer	'And you've done that have you?'
Ryan	'Yeah, that's how I bought Mario 3.'

LA, M, 12 – 13 years

Sometimes children recognised that advertisements rekindled a desire for products, or acted as a reminder:

Gavin	'I bought my Amiga from it [advertisement], I was about to buy it anyway before the advert came but, you know, when you're about to buy it you want it even more.'
Interviewer	'…and you saw the advert and that confirmed your decision?'
Gavin	'It made you more confident.'

MA, M, 10 – 11 years

Children sometimes deliberately refer to advertising when negotiating with parents for things which they want. Indeed, some saw advertisements as a weapon in their armoury of persuasion methods which, in certain circumstances, can be very effective:

Marlon	'I like all these adverts, like if I watch something and I'm always telling my Mum to get me something and my Mum says she's going to get me something, I like ... whenever a TV advert on TV comes on like about TVs and videos I always say that there's one I like.'
Interviewer	'So you use the advert to put pressure on your Mum...?'
Marlon	'Yeah.'
Interviewer	'Do any others of you do that?'
Karl	'Yeah.'

MA, M, 12 – 13 years

Interviewer	'Can you influence them [parents]...?'
Simon	'I try to get them to buy some stuff.'
Anthony	'Usually they do, because it's food ... usually if you say, that looks quite nice, I've seen it on television, they'll probably buy it.'

MA, M, 10 – 11 years

Parents and children shopping together is a marketing opportunity which has not gone ignored by advertisers[7] and, indeed, it seems that children have developed their appreciation of advertising as a tactic with parents from observing the effects of advertising on their parents. Other recent research has shown parental views on advertising can be as influential as the advertisement itself[8] and that parents are also instrumental in the development of a child's consumer attitudes.[9]

Anthony	'My Mum normally buys things from the adverts like washing up powder and things.'
Interviewer	'You think your parents are influenced by adverts on telly?'
Anthony	'Like washing powder. My Dad got butter all over his favourite shirt, so she bought this fat digester one.'
Justin	'Is that Ariel Ultra?'
Anthony	'Something like that.'

MA, M, 10 – 11 years

Children quite often found that once they had bought the product it was not as good as they had anticipated. Their disappointment was often about a food item:

| Thomas | 'Those Push Up [lolly] Pops when they first come, when they were first advertised I thought, "Oh these are going to be right nice", but I didn't like them so much.' |

Craig   'Advertisement went too far, when you stick your finger up, when you sucked it you get all lolly on your finger.'
            LA, M, 10 – 11 years

Marie   'Those McCain Southern Fried Chips, they are supposed to go crunch when you bite them, but they don't … they must have like a sound effect machine in background. And when you bite those green apples, they are supposed to go like, you know what I mean, like a really crisp noise, but they are soggy and they don't make a noise at all.'
            MA, F, 15 – 16 years

Some children, fortunately, had 'viewed' the product after seeing it advertised, but had been disappointed with what they saw:

Henry   'I haven't bought them but I've seen them in the shops, the Stingray things. They look better on the actual TV than they do in the actual boxes. Because you actually see the joins … they don't really show them in the adverts … they look better in the adverts.'
            MA, M, 10 – 11 years

Indeed, this frequently fuelled their cynicism about advertising:

Interviewer 'Do you think that adverts succeed?'
Neil   'I think some do, but most the adverts don't, 'cos you really want to go out and try them first. Like I were thinking about getting a 'B' Battler [computer game], it showed you advert and it were absolutely brilliant, but when I had a look at it, it were just these shields and firing at each other all the time, it were boring.'
            MA, M, 12 – 13 years

It is not possible to determine exactly which advertisements are effective with children and which are not from this research. However, it seems to be a combination of the image which an advert creates, with the opinions or actions of peer group members that ends in a desire for a product:

Neil   'There were these hit sticks where you just have to throw, they were like sticks but they had an amplifier in them so you just had to do that and it played drums, but I'd never played them and I got them 'cos they were on telly and everyone were on about them, that were about two years

	ago, but then just never played on them.'
Interviewer	'Why?'
Neil	''Cos I can't play drums, I just got them 'cos I wanted them.'

MA, M, 12 – 13 years

Among the 15- and 16-year-olds, image seemed to be of primary concern. For the young men, a successful advertisement is likely to be one with which they can personally identify:

Phil	'Like John Barnes, that Lucozade drink, if he drinks it, I will.'
Robbie	'Yeah, I know that Lucozade drink, it's horrible that blue one, in'it?'
Tim	'Yes.'
Robbie	'It is absolutely horrible. Because John Barnes drinks it like for and he kicked that can into that bin and that, I've got to have a drink of that. It's absolutely horrible, it's about 55p and it tastes disgusting.'

MA, M, 15 – 16 years

Young women, however, were often more concerned to disassociate themselves from what they saw as the superficial, stereotypical world that advertising creates. This was often resented:

Interviewer	'What about people in adverts, do you think they're like you...?'
Suzanne	'No, they're not, they're skinny, got really nice hair, they're pretty, perfect figure that like nobody in the world can have.'
Sophie	'They're just too abnormal, they're not normal either are they? I mean you don't normally see someone waggling their heads walking down the street just because they've got a new shampoo ... [laughter] ... they can be short, they can be fat, they can be ugly, it doesn't matter what shampoo they use.'

MA, F, 15 – 16 years

CONCLUSION

Advertisers spend vast amounts of money targeting children and the evidence in this chapter suggests that this is money well spent.[10] Children remember advertisements with great clarity. They differentiate between advertisements as a form of entertainment (as in those where the entertainment value is such that the product is of little relevance) and advertisements that are pertinent to their buying habits. They are aware of the purpose of advertisements but admit to being sometimes influenced by them.

However, a certain scepticism, even cynicism, develops when children are disappointed in the products which they have bought as a result of advertising. Nevertheless, children – especially older ones – admit to spending their 'own' money as a result of advertising, usually on goods that are not too expensive, such as chocolates, sweets, soft drinks, computer games and music cassettes.

Younger children have little spending power in their own right and have to turn to their parents. Like the older children, they consciously use advertising to put pressure on their parents to spend, spend, spend.

In recent years there has been much debate about whether children understand the purpose of advertising and whether there should be more stringent restrictions on advertising directed at children.[11] The evidence in this chapter suggests that, whilst children do understand the purpose of advertising, they continue to be influenced by it. In addition, they are influenced by the opinions of their friends who will, in turn, have been exposed to and, possibly, influenced by advertising.

Further, children from different socio-economic backgrounds watch the same adverts and are influenced by them to a similar extent. Advertising must be, therefore, yet another source of pressure which falls disproportionately on poorer families.

NOTES

1. J H Goldstein, *Television Advertising: a review of research*, Toy Manufacturers of Europe, 1992, pp56-70.
2. Central Statistical Office, *General Household Survey*, HMSO, 1992.
3. R P Adler and R J Faber, 'Background: children's television viewing patterns' in Adler et al, *The Effects of Television Advertising on Children*, Lexington Books, 1980.
4. J U McNeal, *Kids as Customers: a handbook of marketing to children*, Lexington Books, 1992.
5. L K Merinoff and G S Lesser, 'Children's ability to distinguish television commercials from program material', in Adler et al, *op cit*.
6. Cited in Goldstein, *op cit*.
7. See *Journal of Marketing Research 1993*, Volume 33, Number 4.
8. Goldstein, *op cit*.
9. R M Liebert and F Sprafkin, *The Early Window: effects of television on children and youth*, Pergamon Press, 1988.

10. Estimates of advertising expenditure in the 1980s in the US suggest that $6,865,714,000 was spent reaching children. McNeal, *op cit*, p135.
11. Goldstein, *op cit*, pp36–56.

7 'Pretty, pretty, please – just like a parrot': persuasion strategies used by children and young people

Robert Walker, Karl Ashworth, Karen Kellard,
Sue Middleton, Anne Peaker and Michelle Thomas

INTRODUCTION

In previous chapters we have shown the pressures which children experience from friends, school and advertising. Inevitably children translate these pressures into financial demands on parents and others. In this chapter children describe the strategies and tactics which they use in trying to persuade adults to give in to their demands.

Most British studies of the cost of children, certainly those with a policy orientation, have tended to neglect the fact that children are active, not passive, consumers.[1] Advertising and marketing managers have not made the same mistake, and academic research in the US has demonstrated the effectiveness of marketing to children in order to influence their parents.[2]

If such research is to be believed, then the amount that a family spends on children will partially depend on the children's powers of persuasion and their parents' will to resist. Parenting, therefore, is likely to include a series of negotiations between parent and child over the nature and level of the latter's consumption. Moreover, it may well be that it is within these negotiations that the discipline of poverty and the reality of relative deprivation are felt most acutely.

TECHNIQUES

Asked how they would go about getting something that they wanted but could not afford, the children and young people rapidly began to describe a large number of persuasion techniques of varying sophistication.

BEGGING

'Begging' was the most straightforward. Teenage boys resorted to it and it was commonly mentioned by younger children. At its simplest, it involves saying 'please' rather emphatically.

Chris	'Beg 'em. Go on hands and knees!'
Interviewer	'You wouldn't really, would you?'
Jo	'Yeah!'
Interviewer	'…What would you say to them?'
Alex	'Please, pretty, pretty please! Pretty, pretty please!
Jo	'Like a parrot!'
	LA, GU, 8 years

The 'please' may be silent, as when a child stands in front of the desired item in a shop 'looking at it for ages' or keeps returning to the same display window.

In more developed versions, the 'please' is accompanied by a list of reasons why the parent should say 'yes': 'I need it'; 'it's nice'; 'my friend's got one'; 'it's cheap'; 'I'm the only one who hasn't got one'.

Lisa	'I went into a clothes shop and I saw this pair of shorts. They were really nice and I wanted them for when we go away. And I tried them on and I really, really liked them. My Mum said "they're a bit dear, aren't they?" I said "well, I need some shorts for on holiday and everything", and I think I got it through to her head that I wanted them.'
	MA, F, 11 years

REPETITION

Repetition – variously described by children as 'working on them', 'pestering', 'bugging them' – is a key weapon in their arsenal.

Thomas	'Yeah, I'm working on them. Keep asking them, saying "Will you get me a Game Boy for my birthday?" And they keep on saying "Oh wait and see what you'll get".'
	LA, M, 11 years

Children have a clear perception of how repetition works. Parents are put under constant pressure. The only way to escape the pressure is to say 'yes'. When the pressure stops as a result, parents experience a blessed relief.

Interviewer	'What does bugging mean?'
James/	
Christopher	'It gets on their nerves.'
Adam	'You just keep saying it.'
James	'And then when they get it, then you don't bug them any more, do you?'
	LA, M, 13 years

Mixed with flattery, tenacity and a sense of strategy, repetition is seen as a very effective device.

Jane	'I went to the hamster show at school a couple of years ago … and I saw one that I really, really liked. I was pestering him for about four hours on this same day!'
Interviewer	'How did you pester him? What does pestering mean?'
Jane	'It's just sort of like, "Please, I love you Dad. You're the best Dad in the entire world. Oh, go on!" That sort of thing. I just kept pestering and pestering until he finally got sick of me pestering him and went and bought the silly thing.'
	MA, F, 11 years

DIRECT ACTION

Direct action takes a number of forms, more or less illicit, with the common feature of side-stepping parents altogether.

Among teenagers direct action often means buying the item first and informing parents afterwards. The strategy can sometimes backfire if parents disapprove so much that they insist on the item being returned. Also a child has to have the money and be able to shop for themselves.

Marie	'On Saturday, I bought some boots, right, for Christmas off me Nanna, and they are like a pair of Doccers with a right big heel, she made me take them back 'cos she said that they were very unfeminine and I've already got three pairs of Doccers.'
	MA, F, 11 years

Older children also mentioned explicitly creating the apparent need for an item: giving clothes to Oxfam, for example, and then announcing that their wardrobe was empty of clothes.

When children are young enough still to accompany parents shopping, covertly adding goods to the trolley is a frequently mentioned tactic.

Chris   'I pick it up and put it in trolley.'
Interviewer   'And what does your Mum do?'
Chris   'Picks it back out and puts it on the shelf. And then I keep asking her 'til she says, "run back and get one then".'
               LA, GU, 8 years

More illicit, and therefore not surprisingly less frequently mentioned, is the taking of money. As with theft generally, there is the problem of how to explain the sudden appearance of a new item. The eight-year-old quoted below could leave the item at a friend's house but for many children this was seen as an insoluble problem.

Richard   'If your Mum and Dad's out, you can go and sneak and get some money.'
Interviewer   'How would you manage to bring something home?'
Richard   'I wouldn't do that, because they could find it and ask where you got it from. I would have to leave it at Daniel's house or she'd find out I'd bought it.'
               MA, M, 8 years

For the children the probability of being caught was a factor in shop lifting. Some youngsters distinguished between the theft of cheap and expensive items, presumably because they saw different ramifications of being caught. The majority of children and young people ruled out theft, but most did so for pragmatic, as much as for moral, reasons.

Interviewer   'Would you ever do that [steal]?'
Adam   'No.'
Christopher   'It's not worth the risk.'
James   'My brother would.'
Christopher   'If it was something like a chocolate bar or sweets I would. But nothing like computer games.'
               LA, M, 13 years

BRIBERY

Bribery was much more commonly mentioned than theft. In essence, the tactic involves children doing the things that are expected of them (keeping their room tidy, making their bed) but which are less often done in practice, in return for the parent agreeing to a request.

Victoria   'Help Mum more.'

Katherine   'Not jump on your brother.'

Victoria   'Just stuff like keep my bedroom tidy. Not argue with my brother. That's the hardest thing!'

                MA, F, 11 years

Of course, parents recognise this strategy and use it to encourage good behaviour. Even young children, certainly at the age of seven, are well aware of this. Consequently bribery can work symbiotically in the interests of both parties.

Jamie   'I says, "Can I have this Dad?" and he says, "Wait a minute". He looked at it.'

Interviewer 'And what was it?'

Jamie   'Toy aeroplanes.'

Interviewer 'Toy aeroplanes. And it took him a minute to decide did it? Why did he have to think about it?'

Jamie   'He thought about it in case I were naughty.'

Ashley   'Yes, but he behaved, didn't he, so he let him have it.'

                LA, M, 8 years

BARGAINING

Bargaining involves the child offering more than expected good behaviour. It entails doing something rather special: ironing, cleaning the car or washing up. (Some of those children with dishwashers in the home felt that this curtailed their options.)

The strategy, sometimes termed 'creeping', has two permutations. The first, the 'I will if ...' approach, makes the nature of the bargain very explicit. The second relies on more subtle signs aimed at getting the parent in the right frame of mind before popping the question. Tasks are performed unprompted without mentioning the impending request. This can be a high-risk strategy because the parent may not notice. However, the approach is widely canvassed, particularly among older children and young people. Apparently, the parent is often sensitive to the abrupt change in behaviour and, in effect, creates the basis for a bargain by asking the child why s/he is behaving so well.

Both approaches were commonly reported and could be quite sophisticated in their implementation.

Robbie   'Because like I ain't got a Dad. Mum loves it when I show her a right lot of attention. If you just go up to her and go, "Oh, can I have this please, and I'll do a job for yer", then it don't work ... I'll do sommut, let's say, "Oh thanks for that". Then she'll be in a good mood and she'll say to me "Oh what have you done today then?" And then I say, "Oh I went out ... did this, and I saw this". And she'll say, "Oh, yeah, what did you see then? Oh well, you've been good lately and you've done well at school and everything, so I think when I've got a bit o' money together I'll buy you that."'

MA, GU, 15 years

PART-PAYMENT

Another form of bargain involves part-payment and is apparently employed from an early age. The basic model is for the child to offer to contribute to the cost. The precise percentage offered and agreed will depend on the cost of the item and the age and resources of the child.

A variant is for the parents' contribution to take the form of a loan. Sometimes the loan is unsecured. In other cases, it represents an advance of pocket money or the bringing forward of a birthday or Christmas present. Quite commonly the child neither intends nor expects to pay back the loan. Whether parents actively participate in this charade or simply fail to call in their loan through neglect was not established.

NEGOTIATION

Negotiation is the refined high point of the child's portfolio of options. It entails using most, if not all, of the above techniques with consummate skill. Attention is given to strategy, preparation and timing.

Charlotte   'It's dodgy really. It depends on how I went about asking for it. If I wheedle my way around and ask them ... they might take the hint and then just laugh about it and say "Well, because you have taken so much time over it, we might" ... And then, it all depends. It's a fine balance. You have to be skilled. But if I just ask them straight out, they might not let me. It really depends on what mood they are in. You have to pick them at the right time, giving hints, like, "Oh, I saw my

friend and she has this great Game Boy and she has a brand
new game called Tetris and it's really good, and it's got this
really good music". And I'd sing a bit of the music until they
got fed up of that. And then I'd give them another detailed
description of what the Game Boy was like. And do a few
more hints over the next couple of weeks ... Then hopefully
they would take it ... In the end I would just come out with
it "Can I have a Game Boy for my birthday?" And in the
end they might say "Yes".'

> MA, F, 11 years

All the arguments that children feel are likely to appeal to adults are
carefully rehearsed: there is a real need; it is a necessary replacement;
it is cheap but not shoddy; and it is needed for school. As Chapter
Five has shown, this is an ace card with parents.

Simon   'My Mum'll buy me anything for school.'
Anthony   'Anything. If you said, "I need a personal stereo for school",
               she'd probably buy you it!'

> MA, M, 11 years

Negotiation, in its quintessential form, means that some children
claim only to ask for what they know they will get.

THREATS AND ACTIONS

Yet, despite taking painstaking trouble, children admit that they are
not always, or indeed often, successful. (Some of their explanations
for this are reported below.) In such circumstances they have only
one tactic left: anger.

Leah   'Just keep saying "Buy me one please" all the time, 'til she
               said it was alright.'
Interviewer   'What if she said "No"?'
Leah   'I'd just go upstairs and start banging on the floor. That's
               what I do when I'm in a bad mood.'

> MA, F, 11 years

Sometimes anger can be used to great effect. It can even be used as
part of a sophisticated strategy, although children were divided in
their views as to the effectiveness of threats and tantrums. However,
virtually everyone agreed that such actions had been more effective
when they were younger.

Paul	'You could persuade them when you were smaller. Because you cry a lot then. Yes, because my baby brother cries and he always gets what he wants.'
Interviewer	'Really? Why can't you cry then?'
Paul	'We're too old.'
Peter	'They just smack me.'
Paul	'They just start shouting. And when you're small, they buy you things to stop you crying.'

MA, M, 8 years

TARGETS

It is not only parents who come under pressure from children. Who a child approaches probably has much to do with happenstance, but children also make judgements based on their perception of the likelihood of success. They may match the person to the item and vice versa.

Grandparents were mentioned most frequently, usually by younger children, as potential sources of large items. Friends, even other relatives, were unlikely to buy expensive presents. Children recognised that grandparents spoiled them and were not averse to exploiting this.

Paul	'If not, if my Mum and Dad wouldn't let me, and I didn't have enough money, I'd ask my Granddad when my Mum and Dad weren't there.'
Interviewer	'Would you? Do you think he'd say yes?'
Paul	'Yes.'
Interviewer	'What about you. Have you both got Granddads?'
Peter/Matthew	'Yes.'
Interviewer	'Are they easier than your Mum and Dad?'
Paul/Peter	'Yes.'
Matthew	'Much easier.'
Interviewer	'Why is that?'
Peter	'Because they spoil you when you're there.'
Matthew	'Whenever I go to there, we always go the Co-op and we have some sweets and a drink.'
Interviewer	'They're older, you said. Why does that make it easier?'
Peter	'Well they're not young, and young people like shouting and that.'

MA, M, 8 years

There were limits to what grandparents could be expected to afford and these became more significant, or at least were most recognised, among older children, particularly when in their teens. Grandparents could be used to top up savings or even to buy things jointly with parents. Sometimes parents acted as intermediaries in setting up these arrangements.

While children made distinctions according to role, they also took account of personality and circumstance. Some identified particular grandparents whom they considered to be rich, others identified different relatives to whom they could turn if their efforts at persuading parents had come to nought.

Alex   'Me uncle comes with me. I can get anything with me uncle
              but I can't with my Mum.'
              LA, GU, 8 years

Some children also distinguished between parents, and the way in which they approached them – independently and/or together – became a key part of their negotiation strategy. For instance, some choose their mothers for cheap things, and fathers for expensive ones.

One of the mothers involved in another part of the research bemoaned the fact that 'whereas fathers bought the things that children wanted but did not need, mothers bought the things that they needed but did not want'. There is some support for this contention from the children in junior schools who were more than twice as likely spontaneously to mention fathers than mothers as their preferred target. Where a reason was given it was because fathers were more likely to say 'yes'. This may be linked to the perception, quite common among the children, that fathers had more money. (We were, of course, specifically asking children about things that they could not afford to buy themselves and which might, therefore, count as expensive.)

Among the older children, there is a hint of girls turning to their fathers and boys to their mothers, although, as the following extracts (the first involving boys, the second girls) indicate, this is far from being an immutable rule:

Interviewer   ' ...do you always go to your Mum?'
Karl   'Yeah.'
Robert   'Yeah.'
Neil   'Not always...'

Robert	'Well it is easier with my Mum. She gives in easier...'
Michael	'My Dad he likes to spend a lot of money and it is usually my Mum that says "You can't have this with this". But my Dad usually goes "Oh yeah you can have that".'
Interviewer	'You go to your Mum?'
Karl	'Sometimes she buys it and then later on tells my Dad that she's bought it me.'

MA, M, 13 years

Marie	'Mum and Dad.'
Interviewer	'You'd ask your Dad, would you ask your Dad first?'
Marie	'No me Mum first...'
Rachel	'I'd ask me Dad first...'
Rena	'Um, me Dad first.'
Alysia	'I'd ask me Dad first.'

MA, F, 15 years

There were also exceptions and refinements. One 11-year-old boy had a father whom he saw as a good source of sweets but who refused to buy expensive things. A girl of the same age would normally go to her father but not when she wanted clothes, since he hated clothes shopping. A 13-year-old felt that she would go to her father for a track-suit but not for a nightdress.

CONDITIONS

Both children and teenagers recognised that they were not always successful and identified a wide range of factors affecting success. Some factors related to the nature of the request, others to its timing and the family circumstances at the time of the request, another to the skill with which the strategy is implemented.

Children and young people recognise that, other things being equal, their chances of success are much diminished if the desired item is expensive. What counts as expensive differs according to: the type of item; when it is requested (Christmas is the time for big presents); and perhaps age and family circumstance.

However, things are often not equal. If parents disapprove of the cheap item requested – sweets, for example – it may be more productive to ask for something with parent appeal. Indeed, this may be used as a bargaining ploy: a riposte to save up for something better may be accepted, especially if a parental contribution can be extracted.

Parents may accept that expensive items are needed and respond more positively. Indeed, expensive items could arrive unasked for when parents had ulterior motives: they thought it was time the child learned to ride a bike or 'Dad wanted to play the computer game himself'.

Alison   'Well I couldn't ride a bike and my Dad said it was time I learned to ride, so he just bought me one.'
MA, F, 8 years

Joanne   'But if it's a computer game then my Dad will go out and buy it me anyway.'
Leanne   'Yeah, my Dad buys me computer games...'
Emma   'Yeah, the other week I were out and came back in and he was playing on Lemmings which he had just gone out and bought.'
MA, F, 13 years

Children believed that several other features of the request increased the chances of success and would often emphasise them to parents: it was needed; everybody had one; it would stop them being bored; it was needed for school.

Turning to the circumstances of the request, it was widely agreed that the target person had to be in a good mood. Frequently a key part of the strategy was to create this sense of well-being in the potential victim. Hence the attempts at good behaviour, the offers of assistance around the home, presents and 'creeping' generally. There were occasions which could be exploited, when the mother's mind was on other things or even perhaps when she was 'drunk'. There were other times which had to be avoided, typically those when children recognised their parents to be under stress.

Saskia   'She was getting ready to go to work and I just kept saying it and she just said "Wait and see" and I knew she was going to get me one.'
MA, F, 11 years

Nick   'Not when she's watching her favourite television programme.'
Tim   'Or when she's in the car, or when she's driving, she doesn't like driving, so...'
MA, M, 15 years

However carefully children tried to manage the situation, they could not always be sure of the outcome. Beyond the circumstances of the moment, there was the financial situation of the family to be taken into account. The suggestion is that children in more prosperous homes tended to talk of items being 'too expensive', while their counterparts from less prosperous ones reported that their parents 'could not afford' to buy them the thing.[3] The latter seem also to be more aware of fluctuations in domestic finances such that they timed requests not to coincide with weeks in which bills fell due. Children from homes which had suffered a fall in income also seemed particularly sensitive to the financial pressures on their parents.

Joshua   'When they ain't got much money and that. But when they've got the money then it'll be alright … It's just what kind of week it is – if they have to pay bills out and that.'
             LA, M, 15 years

Finally, children and young people were prepared to admit that the chances of success depended on how well they played their hand. Sometimes they made mistakes by not sufficiently preparing the ground or choosing the wrong moment to pose the request.

Jane   'If you don't ask them the right way. If it just sounds as if you're being ungrateful and everything, and you know, you've got loads of things already and they say, honestly, you've got so many clothes your wardrobe's going to be clogged up.'
             MA, F, 11 years

AGEING, AUTONOMY AND REGRETS

The range of persuasion techniques used by eight-year olds was already large and scarcely altered after the age of eleven. Likewise, there is not much evidence from the groups that older children apply such techniques with greater sophistication than 11-year-olds, although this might reflect increased reticence among teenagers to explain their tactics to an adult. On the other hand, they are more often prepared to admit that their efforts are unsuccessful, which could indicate a more realistic assessment of their performance. However, the teenagers would argue that they are less successful now than when they were younger. They offer a set of intuitively plausible reasons.

As teenagers, they typically receive more pocket money than when they were younger. As a consequence, they have a greater capacity to buy what they want and their parents know this. Moreover, they are often expected to meet the cost of an increased range of items from their pocket money – by now commonly termed an allowance, clothes money, spending money, etc. Therefore the number of things which they could confidently expect their parents to purchase is much reduced.

Michelle   'If it's just little things they make you buy it yourself.'
Debbie   'Yeah.'
Michelle   'If it's too big they say it's too expensive.'
Debbie   'They just don't like paying for you when you're older, my Mum and Dad don't anyway.'
Interviewer 'Why not?'
Debbie   'Because they think you're old enough to look after yourself.'
             LA, F, 15 years

Furthermore, even before young people reach the age of 16, their parents often expect them to fund their purchases by part-time employment. In practice, not many of the teenagers did work regularly, although a number of the young men still did paper-rounds, while the young women worked Saturdays in shops and could earn money baby-sitting. Parents can always deny a request for money with the riposte that their offspring should get a job.

Joshua   'If I was a little kid and wanted to have things ... they bought things. But now they say "Oh, you should go out to work and get a part-time job and get your own money".'
             LA, M, 15 years

The young people also reported wanting more expensive things than when they were younger. This means that parents are less prepared to contribute straightaway, if at all. They are perhaps also more likely to look for a financial contribution from their children. Moreover, the sheer expense of items may rule out alternative sources of finance that were once important. Grandparents are a case in point. When young, children could look to grandparents for the second largest present at Christmas. While this might still be true, teenage aspirations can outstrip grandparents' ability to deliver, especially if the grandparents have retired. On the other hand, some teenagers may be able to turn to older siblings for financial, as well as moral, support.

Interviewer 'Do you actually give up if your Mum says she won't buy it for you.'

Layla   'If my sister's down town she says "Come on, I'll get it for you" ... She's always buying me stuff ... trainers, tops, clothes and stuff.'

               LA, F, 13 years

As a result of having resources of their own, coupled with the ability to increase those resources through paid work, young people may gain in self-esteem and financial autonomy. But these gains are, to some extent, offset by the partial withdrawal of parents as a source of extra cash. Moreover, even the financial autonomy that young people enjoy is only partial, in that parents still want to know where they have been, and what they have done with the money. Parents continue to make clear what they approve and disapprove of and seek to enforce those views.

Marie   'They don't know that I drink, and I don't smoke and I don't take drugs so...'

Interviewer   'So it is quite easy to really spend your money on what you want?'

Marie   'I just say, "I've been in McDonalds", that's the easiest place.'

Sophie   'Spend it on what I want. But then she always asks "Where has it gone?" and she always says "If you're buying booze and you're buying cigarettes, then I'm gonna kill yer".'

               MA, F, 15 years

Teenagers may be rather more aware than their younger siblings of the financial pressures on parents from other quarters. Occasionally they mentioned 'feeling guilty' about asking for money and knew about the dire financial straits some of their parents were in.

Suzanne   '...you're not scrounging off them all the time. Like my Mum's always saying to me ... can I get a Saturday job? I'll be able to get part-time work when I've finished me exams. Then it won't be, "Mum lend us a tenner, lend us a fiver", like all the time. But she won't say "Go out and find a job 'cos you're not having no money off me".'

               MA, F, 15 years

Sharon   'My Dad talks to me more about "we're in debt", or whatever. He talks to me more about it now 'cos I understand it. So I'm not gonna say "I need some new shoes, I need some new clothes, a new coat, as well, while you're at it!".'

               MA, F, 15 years

Whereas children of all ages mentioned saving as a strategy, only among the oldest groups was this ever seen as the principal or sole available strategy. The older groups were also more likely to accept, or to admit to accepting, a 'no' from their parents and to not pushing their requests too far.

Lauren   'If they haven't got much money then they can't buy anything, but if they have, then I ask. I know when my Mum's got some money.'
LA, F, 11 years

Interviewer   'Do you reckon you can persuade your parents?'
Lee   'No. If it's your Mum and she says "What do you want? No you can't have it".'
Tim   'I can persuade me Mum, but not me Dad.'
Nick   'I can when they're on their own, like, either me Mum or me Dad, but once they get together talking, like, no chance.'
MA, M, 15 years

Even the youngest groups felt that they could no longer resort to tantrums and other forms of direct action to put pressure on their parents. Likewise, teenagers watched their younger siblings succeed where they no longer could. Indeed, it was partly the success of siblings, their very presence, that eroded the resources coming to them.

Debbie   'Because my brother's seven years younger than me, so I used to get all I wanted until he popped up, and now I don't...'
Michelle   'Me, Debbie and Steven are close ages. Debbie always got what she wanted. Well, she still does. She was off school just because she hurt her foot.'
Interviewer   'The rest of you said it was easier when you were younger. Why was that?'
Debbie   'I don't know, because you're cute when you're young, aren't you?'
LA, F, 8 years

However, this is not to say that teenagers stop pressurising their parents for money. They mentioned using all the strategies adopted by younger children and one or two others as well. Notably, because they had resources of their own, they could afford to buy parents presents in the confident expectation that one expenditure would stimulate another bigger one in return.

Claire	'I'd go "M...u...m, I've seen something really nice". Sometimes I'd get her some flowers, 'cos my Mum really likes flowers.'
Interviewer	'Does that work though?'
Rebecca	'I go to the shop and buy my Mum something and she'll buy me something.'
	MA, F, 11 years

EFFECTIVENESS AND CONSEQUENCES

The children and young people to whom we listened were able to give detailed descriptions of the tactics and strategies that they use to persuade their parents to buy them things that they want. Most consider themselves to be modestly successful.[4] Advertisers would therefore seem to have got it right, while policy analysts may have been ignoring something quite important. Indeed, there is a striking similarity between the techniques reported by these British children and those described in the US: pleading, persistent, forceful, demonstrative, sugar-coated, threatening and pity ('everyone has one but me').[5]

The bribery, negotiations and coercion described were seen as being a normal part of daily life, irrespective of socio-economic background or household composition. There were hints in the discussions that children from less affluent homes were more prone to report simple repetition and anger, especially when young, and direct action than were their contemporaries from more affluent homes. Children living with one parent may also have a different perspective. Certainly they are usually unable simultaneously to play one parent off against another, although when there is contact with an absent parent this provides a rather special target to 'work on'. The evidence in the US is that children of lone parents assume more of the role of partner and handle money at an earlier age.[6] In the groups they more often mentioned buying presents for their parents.

The direct action of children from poorer homes may reflect financial constraints rather than simply a lack of negotiating skills. It is clear from Chapter Two that children share a fairly common culture of acquisition while, in the groups, children from less affluent areas were more likely to report their parents not having the money and were perhaps more sensitive to the need to avoid requests in weeks when bills fell due. It may be that the tantrums, shouting and door-banging to which they resort is one domestic manifestation of relative deprivation. Low-income parents, especially mothers, make great sacrifices to protect their children from the indignities of poverty.[7] To escape the trauma of remorseless 'bugging' may be one of the reasons why.

NOTES

1. A rare exception is: M Hill, 'Children and money', *Benefits*, Issue 3, January/February 1992.
2. J U McNeal, *Kids as Customers: a handbook of marketing to children*, Lexington Books, 1992.
3. It is planned to examine this and other findings in a national survey of expenditure on children which will include a ten-minute interview with children.
4. Parents, it should be said, believe that children are much less successful than they claim, but agree that they are often put under pressure.
5. McNeal, *op cit*, pp73-4.
6. McNeal, *ibid*, p7.
7. For example, see B Dobson, A Beardsworth, T Keil, R Walker, *Diet, Choice and Poverty*, Family Policy Studies Centre (forthcoming).

8 Saying 'No' or giving in gracefully

Sue Middleton and Michelle Thomas

Chapter Seven has described the multifarious persuasion strategies which children use in negotiating with parents and others to satisfy their financial demands. Parents have two options when dealing with such demands: either to give in or to say 'no'.

What parents choose to do will depend on a number of factors: whether they can afford it; whether they approve of the requested item; and, more generally, whether they consider it good for the child to have what s/he wants at any particular point in time. In this chapter we describe the reasons which parents give for limiting their children's demands and the efforts which they make to resist pressure, how and to what parents say no, and the compromises which they reach with their children in 'giving in gracefully'. In particular, we show how poorer parents are restricted in their negotiating options and the likely impact of these restrictions on their children.

THE IMPORTANCE OF SETTING LIMITS

Parents are very aware of the materialistic pressures on children but also of the need to teach children that they cannot have everything they want, even if the family can afford it. Obviously, the smaller the family budget the greater the limits which have to be imposed on children's demands. However, it is clear that better-off parents are equally as concerned to limit their children's demands as less well-off parents, although their reasoning is somewhat different. Parents from the lowest socio-economic groups need their children to understand the limitations of the family budget from an early age.

Felicity (3)   ''cause I think they tend to be spoilt enough, you know so they've got to learn what no means – "no".'
11 – 16 years

Lorraine (3)   'I have to bring them up so that they know they can't have it. I always explain to them that I can't afford it.'
0 – 5 years

Better-off parents tend to justify limiting their children's demands on the grounds that it is intrinsically good for them not to get everything they want.

Emma (1)   'But I think in the long run it would help, I think it would work to their benefit to actually explain week after week the benefit of not giving in, not becoming one of the sheep and being pressurised into having something that everybody else has, not developing their individuality...'
11 – 16 years

Jackie (1)   'I want them to be thrilled by what they get at birthdays and Christmas. I remember a present that my Dad bought me when I was seven which was the only present that I was ever bought outside birthdays and Christmas and I still remember it and I don't want to devalue the others. It's not that I'm mean but I don't think that children should have too many things in between.'
0 – 5 years

Better-off parents were also the most vocal in their determination to resist peer group pressure, both from other children and other mothers, while less well-off parents were more inclined to regret and feel guilty about their inability to give their children what they want.

June (2)   'On a good day you know what you think about spending £50 on a pair of trainers for a ten-year-old – you know that it's not reasonable ... but most people can't afford it, and as long as you keep that in your mind when your children say "everyone else at school has a pair". You know that they don't, because you know that everyone can't be wearing £50 trainers because people can't afford to buy them. You've got to keep that strength in yourself not to be conned by your children saying everybody has them, because you know everybody doesn't.'
6 – 16 years

Rona (3)   'I think you say "no" when you really haven't got it don't
              you? But you're sorry.'
              11 – 16 years

Despite these divergences in attitudes between families with different
levels of financial resources, there was widespread agreement about
the importance of all children learning limits. Some mothers felt that
this should start at a very early age.

Stephanie (2)   'No, but he's got to learn, so even if I give him 50p he'll
                know that if he goes into a shop he can't buy something for
                £5 because he hasn't got enough. Whereas before we'd say,
                "Well, okay, we'll treat you", now we sort of say "Well no".
                He's got to learn some way.'
                2 – 5 years

Others felt the teenage years to be particularly important, since this is
a time when failure to impose limits and resist peer pressure can lead
to other, more dangerous, activities.

Alison (2)   'Because as adults you can't have some of what your neigh-
               bours have and I think it's part of growing up and I think that
               the teenage years are the time when reality has to set in.
               Otherwise they'll be influenced into all sorts of things. If you
               allow it to go on too far with clothes, the next thing is drugs
               and all sorts of things.'
               11 – 16 years

Having made the decision to set limits, parents have to be prepared
to resist the sophisticated persuasion strategies and tactics employed
by children (described in Chapter Seven). They have two alternatives:
to say 'no' and stick to it, or to find a satisfactory compromise – what
we have described as 'giving in gracefully'.

PARENTS' RESISTANCE

Parents described their strategies for resisting children's demands. These
ranged from refusing, through making promises for the future which
they had no intention of fulfilling, to giving a detailed explanation of
the reasons for the refusal.

Sharon (3)   'I just say, "not today".'
               6 – 16 years

Helen (3)   'I do tend to sometimes say, if they're having a bit of a paddy, you know, "next week", or, if we're in "A" shop, I say, "well, wait until we're in "B" shop, it's cheaper". Things like that, to put it off.'

0 – 5 years

Linda (1)   'Well, you just say, "yeah, okay", and then when it comes to it you don't buy it'.

6 – 10 years

Alison (2)   'I explained that it was a lot of money and I wasn't prepared to pay that amount of money. I said, "you could probably have two or even three pairs, which are just as good quality for the same money". He was disappointed and I think he understood the reasoning behind it, but he still would have liked them, you know.'

11 – 16 years

These strategies differed starkly according to economic circumstances. Better-off parents are able to set consistent limits on particular demands which can be explained to the children and, hence, cause less problems because fewer limits have to be set. For poorer families, limits have to be more generic and are often applied less consistently, since what cannot be afforded one week might be possible next week.

Jackie (1)   'Even with the five-year old I can direct him into what he wants which are things which I want him to have. To a certain degree I know his likes and dislikes but there's no way ... I mean I just look at some of the boys' toys and I just think that they're so revolting and luckily because he doesn't see these things on the telly he doesn't want these things.'

0 – 5 years

Kathie (3)   'If I've got it they get it, if I haven't got it, it's, "No, not this week".'

11 – 16 years

The specific items to which parents say 'no' varied little with economic circumstances, although better-off parents were slightly more likely to describe restrictions on sweets, toys and computers, whereas poorer parents tended to talk about restrictions on clothes.

Carole (1)   'No sweets.'
Melanie (1)   'No silly toys.'

Jane (1)   'No rubbish.'
              6 – 16 years

Sandra (1)   'I've managed to say no because he hasn't got one [a computer]
              ... because I've seen the way they can get addicted to it ... Plus
              I have a nephew that gets epileptic fits and having heard this
              could be it, the longer I can keep them away from it the better.'
              6 – 10 years

Lorraine (3) 'My daughter wants fashionable things and she's nearly nine.
              But designer labels – she's got no chance and she knows it.
              There's no way I'm going to buy £30 trainers when I can
              get them for about £5 or £6.'
              0 – 5 years

However, all parents were extremely reluctant to refuse to buy anything
which they considered to be educational. This reinforces the evidence
in Chapter Five about the emphasis which parents place on educational
participation. It also shows that children have correctly identified
education as the weak point in their parents' armoury of resistance, as
described in Chapter Seven.

Sally (2)   'If we're out and the kids ask for books, then I'll always buy
              books. If I think it's educational then I'll buy it. If it's just, "I
              want this and I want that, I want this doll", just because
              they've seen it, then I won't buy it. So for me, my kids have
              got more jigsaws and books and things than little dinky toys
              that they've just seen and got their eyes on. And paints, you
              know, I'll not refuse to buy paints or paper or creative things.'
              2 – 5 years

Lauren (3)   'I think the ones they're doing with school like museums and
              ... it's part of the school work so that to me is essential.'
              11 – 16 years

Sharon (1)   'I do spend a lot of money on books because I would rather
              her be upstairs in her room on a Saturday afternoon reading a
              book than sat in front of a video I suppose. So because of
              that I'm prepared maybe to go down to "C" shop and spend
              £12 a month on books which she'll read if I buy them ...
              To me that is money well spent.'
              6 – 16 years

Despite the need for poorer parents to refuse more often, most parents emphasised the importance of always explaining to children why they are saying no. The sophistication of the explanation given varies from a simple 'I can't afford it', to more extensive training in the realities of the family budget.

Selena (2)   '...it wasn't long after his Father died and I said, "Yes, G, but out of this money I have to pay this and this and this", and I don't believe in telling your children all your business, but he was asking these questions so I did start saving my receipts from the shop, and I did start presenting him with these bills, and he said, "Oh, Mummy, how do you manage?"'
              6 – 16 years

Some parents attempt to get their children to resist the pressures of advertising, with varying degrees of success.

Jenny (1)   'I talk about the advertising with my children because they come up and tell me how marvellous x, y and z is, and you say, "Is it really that good? Let's think about it. Someone's trying to make a lot of money." And I really thought I was getting somewhere until my child said, "Yes, they do tell you lies don't they 'cause we all know that Flash is the best".'
             0 – 5 years

It is also apparent that children from poorer families are taught about the limitations of the family budget at a very early age and that parents rely on children's understanding of the circumstances in limiting their demands.

Liz (3)   'I'm a single parent and because he's never had it he doesn't say, "Oh, my mate's got this, my mate's got the other". I mean, he has said that he'd like a new computer for Christmas but he's been told he's got no chance. I mean, he won't keep going on about it, he's quite good really.'
           6 – 10 years

Lorraine (3)   'I've brought her up like that and she knows that there's no way she's going to get anything like that [a school holiday abroad]. I haven't got the money.'
                0 – 5 years

Poorer parents believe that their children learn not to ask for things which they know their parents cannot afford.

Laura (3)   'They've been very good, they've never bothered, they've

never bothered at all.'
6 – 10 years

Vicky (3) 'But there are ways round things aren't there with children, and they do understand that Mum's struggling and they haven't got the money, and they're not like other people.'
6 – 16 years

Yet evidence from our work with children suggests that those from less well-off families do aspire to the same possessions as their peers. It may be that, far from limiting their economic aspirations, children are simply keeping them suppressed and hidden when at home. This is borne out by parents' descriptions of children's reactions to having their demands turned down. Better-off parents describe lengthy arguments and persistent pressure from children, whereas poorer parents refer to short sulks and tantrums which they believe decrease rapidly as children get older and understand budget limitations.

Anna (3) 'So there are certain things that you draw the line at. I mean they probably fall out with you and get the hump with you for the night but the next day they'll realise that yes you were talking sense.'
11 – 16 years

Interviewer 'What do they do if you don't get them what they want?'
June (3) 'Just have a tantrum.'
0 – 5 years

Frances (1) 'Well, my boy came home with the cruise one and I said "no way", and he said, "well, you've got two years". I said "I still can't afford £10 per week". Then he came home with the skiing one and his face was bright 'cause he thought, well, that's half the price, and I said "well, I still can't afford it". And the Euro Disney one, he came home with that and said "I told them you might be able to afford this one" 'cause it had dropped even further and I felt awful. So what I did in the end, there was a few places left and they put their names in the hat and I thought he'll never get picked, there are so many of them. So I said, "okay you can put your name in the hat", but he got picked, so I had to save money for that one.'
11 – 16 years

Some parents emphasised the importance of saying 'no' and sticking to it and the advantages which this brings.

Janice (1)   'These things that I just won't let mine do and when others are doing it I find it very hard but I stick to my guns and it's paying dividends. Definitely paying dividends being firmer.'
    11 – 16 years

However, for many, particularly the better-off, parents, a refusal is simply a first gambit in a lengthy and complex process of negotiations which often involves giving in to demands or, as they would put it, reaching a compromise. After all, saying 'no' to children is not easy.

Glenys (3)   'Everybody wants, I don't care whatever their income, you all want to give your child the best you possibly can. But there comes that limit, you know you just can't do it. But I don't know how you say no ... where do you stop?'
    11 – 16 years

GIVING IN GRACEFULLY

Very few parents were prepared to admit that they give in to their children's demands and those that did felt guilty about their lack of determination.

Sylvia (1)   'I feel guilty sometimes because I've got an elder daughter and she never had half as much spent on her as the second one ... Sometimes I do think that my daughter maybe has clothes too easily. I see something and I might think about the pennies but if I really like it she usually gets it, even if I wait a few weeks or something. Sometimes I think about it and I know that I don't want her to have it come too easy. I want to try and get her to save.'
    6 – 16 years

However, despite their general unwillingness to admit openly to giving in, it is apparent that most parents do have strategies which they bring into play to allow their children to have at least some of what they want, without their being seen to give in. All these strategies are underpinned by a belief that their use will teach children valuable lessons about 'real life'.

Caroline (1)   'I think they've got to learn from the start, they've got to choose what's their priority because that's what it's going to be all your life, isn't it – what's your priorities?'
    11 – 16 years

These strategies for compromising with children fall into three main types: getting children themselves to prioritise and choose between their demands; making children contribute from their 'own' money; and giving children a degree of financial autonomy. Again, it must be emphasised that better-off parents were able to employ more of these strategies more frequently. Less well-off parents often cannot afford to compromise, as was shown by the limited role played by these parents in the group discussions on these issues.

Making children choose or prioritise from a range of wants begins at an early age, usually in the context of clothes.

Ann (2)   'Obviously I don't let him have a free rein in the shop and say choose whatever you like. I select two jumpers and say "which one of these do you like best?"'

             0 – 5 years

This strategy is employed by all parents, whatever their economic circumstances. However, it tends to be used by poorer parents as a means of limiting expenditure while, for better-off parents, giving the child some choice is seen as important in itself.

Terry (3)   'Let them pick out what you can afford. You don't go into a shop where there's things that you can't afford so you go and show them and say, "Now, which one?".'

             0 – 5 years

Ann (2)   'I find that if M's had some choice in what he's wearing he's going to wear it more willingly than if I bought it because I like it and he doesn't like it.'

Sally (2)   'I think you should let them have a say anyway.'

             0 – 5 years

As children get older, the pressure on parents to pay for a range of activities increases. Again, rather than refusing, parents make their children prioritise, but, depending on the financial circumstances of the family, for very different reasons.

Interviewer   'Is there anything she's asked to do that you've said no to?'

Melanie (1) 'Horse-riding.'

Interviewer   'Because of the expense?'

Melanie (1) 'Well, she's doing enough already. She has music lessons and dancing lessons.'

             6 – 16 years

Helen (3)   'You have to meet them half way. I said to my daughter she can't go horse-riding, she can't have modelling lessons because I haven't got the money. But she goes to ballet and she has swimming lessons.'
            0 – 5 years

Parents also start to expect older children to contribute to the cost of certain items or activities from their 'own' money. A wide range of things were described to which older children are expected to contribute, from deodorant and shampoo through to foreign holidays with school.

Glenda (3) 'I think it must be better with girls because they buy ever such a lot themselves. You know, their own make-up, their own this and that, their own hair lacquer, they buy all that themselves.'
            11 – 16 years

Eve (1)   'She wants to go to Italy with the school. We've said, "Yes, but you've got to contribute towards it". Which she's happy to do and she's saving for it and it's giving her an aim to have something to save for.'
            11 – 16 years

However, children were most often expected to contribute towards the cost of clothing items which they wanted but which parents were either unwilling or unable to pay the total cost. This proved to be the main means by which parents deal with the pressure for designer label clothes and shoes. Again, poorer parents cannot afford them, whereas better-off parents refuse to pay on principle.

Rona (3)   'My son has what I can afford … what I spend on my youngest son, I give my eldest son towards his designer label and say, "If you want designer you buy it".'
            11 – 16 years

Linda (1)   'My son went and bought him some Nike [trainers]. £70 they were, reduced to £50, he used his birthday money on them.'
Interviewer 'But you wouldn't pay it?'
Linda (1)   'No I wouldn't. On principle.'
            6 – 10 years

Parents justify such compromises on the grounds that children are learning invaluable lessons about budgeting and saving which they sometimes learn the hard way.

Amanda (2)   'My son learnt a very good lesson by wanting a Game Gear very badly because everybody else had it, and he had quite a lot of birthday and Christmas money, so I said, 'Okay, if you want to spend it on that, do so'. And he did and I said he'd only play with it for a couple of weeks and, sure enough, a couple of weeks and that was it. And he realised that it was his money, he'd spent it and he could have spent it on something else, and it was a very good lesson to him.'

        6 – 16 years

Making children use their 'own' money also forces them to decide what they really want, as opposed to what they would like, thereby helping parents to limit their expenditure.

Adrienne (2)   'I think in a way it works out cheaper giving pocket money, because otherwise every time you pick them up from school, "Mum can I have this, can I have that?" And you say, "Have you got any pocket money left?" "No, I've spent it". "Well, you're not having it then".'

June (2)   'It also sorts out what they really want as well. My children will say, "Can I have this?" and I'll say they can go and buy it, and they'll say, "With my money?", and I'll say yes, and they don't bother then. So they don't really want it. They don't want it badly enough to spend their money anyway.'

        6 – 16 years

While some older children do earn and contribute from paper rounds or baby-sitting, most often children's 'own' money has been given to the child as a present or given directly by the parents in the form of pocket money. Parents disagree as to whether children should have to 'earn' pocket money by doing jobs around the house.

Doreen (2)   'I employ my older daughter so she saves up for a lot of her own clothes. She wanted a job, I wanted a cleaner, 'cause I work full-time, so she does the cleaning and I pay her and she saves up for her own clothes.'

Roz (1)   'I find that there's a certain amount of chores that my boys are expected to do because they're part of the family, but then there are things that I wouldn't expect them to do but they can earn for doing if they want to.'

        11 – 16 years

Whether children are expected to 'earn' their pocket money or not, it is interesting that most parents do not seem to recognise that this is still part of the family budget which they are allocating to their children. However, poorer parents are only too well aware of this and, as a result, are less likely to be able to afford to give their children regular pocket money. They are aware that their children are missing out on learning how to manage money, but simply cannot afford the risk of money being wasted. They cannot allow their children the freedom to learn from their mistakes.

Samantha (3)   'I always feel guilty that he ought to have learnt how to save money and budget for himself, but I tried several times to give him pocket money but I've just seen it wasted so I've stopped.'

Chris (1)   'My two, they budget their money, they know what they've got. I mean, I give S pocket money and she puts it in her purse and she's going like this with her fingers and I'm saying, "How much have you got there?" "£35", she says, and she's so chuffed because she's been saving it all up.'

11 – 16 years

The third strategy which parents employ to limit their children's demands as they grow older is an extension of pocket money into a weekly or monthly 'allowance'. Children are expected to use this allowance to cover some of their expenditures. The types of expenditure and the amount of the allowance vary from family to family. Some mothers hand over child benefit to the child and expect the child to buy all her/his clothes and pay for all her/his activities and entertainment. Others give a smaller amount to cover sweets and entertainment. Parents believe this to be an invaluable part of growing up and learning to manage money, as well as a means of limiting their children's demands.

Caroline (1)   'I've stopped spending money. They don't have that any more, they just have their family allowance. I've said, "That's your clothing allowance and ... if you spend it all in one week then you go without". Then they know when you get a wage if you spend it all in the first week you've got nothing left.'

11 – 16 years

Sonia (2)   'She has to be very wary of it, because if it comes back and I disapprove of it, it has to go back. And she's learnt the lesson, she has to face the shop and say, "No, this is rubbish, I'm not allowed to have it", but it's the way she's learnt she's got to get value for money, and it's got to be serviceable.'

6 – 16 years

Amanda (2)   'I've just started doing that with my son who's 12, and I don't give him a full clothing allowance because I don't think it's necessary, but I give him a reasonable amount of pocket money and I expect him to budget for certain things ... if he wants something he has to save up for it, if he's got a birthday of a pal, he'll save up for his friend's birthday ... It was actually costing me a fortune before. It was, "I need so and so. Can I go to the cinema? Can I go...?" and I suddenly thought, "This is getting out of hand".'

6 – 16 years

Poorer parents, however, cannot afford to take the risks which would be involved in giving their children this financial education.

Caroline (1)   'I've started letting mine have their family allowance. Once a month they get their family allowance and I'm doing it on a six-month basis and I bought them shoes and coats and the main stuff beforehand, and I've said "Anything you buy, you've got to buy it out of your family allowances". And I'm doing that just so they know what things cost ... So they get thirty odd pounds each a month and that's for them to go out and buy their clothes.'

Denise (3)   'I've got to do something like that but I don't think I can afford it now. I don't give her spending money for anything at all.'

11 – 16 years

In this chapter we have shown how parents set limits on their children's demands, either by saying 'no' or by reaching a compromise. Such compromises can involve parents giving in to demands. However, they justify giving in because they feel that their children learn some invaluable lessons in economics in the process. Children from poorer families are doubly disadvantaged in this respect: first, their parents are forced to refuse more frequently, to more requests, but with less consistency because of the week-to-week uncertainties of the family finances. Financial discipline is exerted from necessity, rather than any decision about what it is good or bad for the child to have or do. Second, their parents cannot afford the risk of waste involved in giving children financial autonomy in order that they can learn the budgeting strategies which, as Chapter Nine will show, their parents employ to such good effect. Poorer parents believe that their children understand the realities of the family's financial circumstances and, because they have learnt not to ask, that children accept that they cannot have access to the same things as their wealthier peers. Evidence from our work with children suggests that this is not the case – children share a common culture of acquisition, whatever the financial circumstances of their families. It seems, therefore, that because they do not have the freedom to learn practical budgeting skills at first hand, poorer children begin to experience the reality of relative deprivation at a very early age. They learn not to ask and how to go without.

9 Budgeting for survival: strategies and support

Sue Middleton and Michelle Thomas

INTRODUCTION

In the first six chapters of this book we described how the economic demands of children combine with external pressures in a manner which must inevitably strain all but the largest of family budgets. Chapters Seven and Eight described the negotiating strategies and tactics which children employ to get what they want, and which parents use to resist and/or limit their children's demands. However, once these negotiations are complete, parents are still left to manage the competing demands on the family budget.

Families have three alternatives in trying to make ends meet: to increase the pot of resources available; to make resources go further; or to refuse certain demands on resources. This chapter describes how families draw on sources outside the immediate family to increase the family budget and some of the strategies used to meet the demands of children within that budget. Chapter Ten examines how these strategies are implemented in relation to child benefit – an element of the family budget which is fixed for all families.

INCREASING FAMILY RESOURCES

The nuclear family consisting of Mum, Dad and 2.4 children, living on their own in isolation from traditional family and community networks has informed much of the conventional wisdom about modern family life. Some politicians and pundits parade the notion of a 'golden age', now firmly in the past, when Granny looked after the children, older children 'looked out for' their younger siblings and the whole community shared responsibility for each other and, particularly, for children. It is suggested that, if we could only return to this, many of society's problems would be solved at a stroke. For example, most recently, the suggestion has been advanced of requiring single mothers to have recourse to their own parents for financial support, rather than to the state.

The clear message from this study is that wider family and community support, far from being a long-dead historical ideal, remains crucial to the financial survival of many families in Britain today.

Sue (3)   'I couldn't do without them.'

Anita (3)   'I've still got my dear little Mum, who is an OAP, and she sends me £10, once in a blue moon, but she can't afford to, and it's so sweet of her, it makes me cry when she does that … It's like families looking after their own isn't it?'

Sue (3)   'My Mum is still on her own, but she works all the hours God sends just to make sure my children don't go without anything, in a sense she's got rid of me, but she's taken them on as her own.'

Anita (3)   'That's good, without your family and friends, what have you got?'

0 – 5 years

Support from family and friends takes many forms, from direct purchases and financial provision for the children to baby-sitting. However, different family members and friends provide different types of support.

Grandparents tend to provide additional finance, and high-cost goods and services, although among less well-off families they can be relied on for basics. Children in families at either end of the economic spectrum receive money directly from grandparents, both regular small amounts for pocket money or savings and larger amounts for Christmas and birthdays.

Joanne (1)   'Andy's Mum, the Grandparents, they've opened an account for them. They don't put 50p to the price of hankies but they put 50p a week in and since they've been born it's added up.'

11 – 16 years

Leslie (3)   'I live with my parents. My mother gives her money, but she

doesn't give her pocket money, she puts a couple of pounds in the building society.'
11 – 16 years

Sally (1)   'Easter, birthdays and holidays they [grandparents] send her money.'
6 – 16 years

Grandparents also supply high-cost items, from 'one-off' items at birth such as prams and pushchairs, to expensive clothing items such as winter coats and shoes.

Angela (2)   'Granddad pays for all of their shoes, that was his present to us when they were born, he would pay for every pair while he was alive so that is all right. I mean we still have to pay out on the day but when we go home he gives us the money, it is quite good because you spend what you want on them because he's retired.'
0 – 5 years

This mother aroused a great deal of envy among her colleagues in the group, particularly from the one mother who did not have family upon whom she could rely.

Ann (2)   'You were quite lucky then. You see, I had to buy everything because me and N are the only ones on his side of the family and on mine that's got children.'
0 – 5 years

Grandparents are often the only possible source of family holidays, trips and treats, the 'extras' which mothers believed to be so important to their children's ability to lead a full life.

Sharon (3)   'I've had three [sic] holidays this year … I went to Yarmouth twice, and up to Scotland twice. It was cold … My Mum and Dad and S's Mum and Dad paid every time … We didn't have to pay for it, just spending money.'
6 – 16 years

However, some mothers wished that they had more control over grandparents' spending, either because they were concerned that the grandparents were spoiling children or, more importantly, because the family had more pressing needs on which the money could have been better spent.

Sandy (3)	'I was awful because they spent £3,000 on this holiday for me and the kids and...'
Sue (3)	'All she did was moan because she needed a washing machine.'
Sandy	'I really needed the washer.'
Anita (3)	'I can understand that.'
Sue	'I would have said to my Mum, "Mum, I need a washer, I don't need a holiday" and my Mum would have got me the washer instead.'
Sandy	'My Mum and Dad had already paid for the holiday and my Mum sat there and explained that they've got money in the bank, but that's for emergencies, and they've only got that much to spend, and I thought, I still want a washing machine.'
	6 – 16 years

In contrast to grandparents, friends and aunts and uncles are relied upon less for direct financial, large-scale support than for help with childcare and the passing on of 'hand-ons'. Mothers clearly discriminated between these goods, which come from someone they know and are, therefore, acceptable, and second-hand goods, whose antecedents are unknown and thus much less tolerable.

Jackie (2)	'...depends where it comes from ... friends ... very good friends. I wouldn't just have them from anybody or buy them. I'd never go to a second-hand shop.'
	6 – 10 years

The rule seems to be that, except for underpants, socks and shoes, any handed-on item is acceptable.

Karen (3)	'To be honest, I'm always dubious of any clothes that come into direct contact with the body, I don't know why it is, but you wonder where ... I don't know it's just something about that, I just wouldn't think of buying something second hand.'
	6 – 10 years

Hand-ons, both from older children and from the wider family and friends, are a major means of supplementing the family resources. Mothers described receiving a whole range of goods from family and friends which, while important to the budgets of all families, played a different role according to socio-economic status. Better-off families tend to use hand-ons as windfalls to be used in addition to their own purchases for the child whereas, for low-income families, hand-ons are often the only way in which they can afford to clothe their children.

Samantha (1)   'I get a lot passed down from my sister because she has got one that's a little bit older, but even so I was still surprised at how much I had spent, because I don't think, even though she hands them down, it doesn't stop me buying, I think I buy probably as much as I would anyway, because they're not always my choice.'
               2 – 5 years

Wendy (3)   'The only new thing mine have got is the bed, their beds. Everything else is either passed down from what I've had or from my family or from friends.'
               6 – 10 years

Friends set up networks for the exchange of hand-ons, circulating items between mothers as children are born and grow up. The conversation between these two mothers, each of whom was expecting her second child, was typical.

Naomi (3)   'Can you ask D if she wants to sell her steam steriliser?'
Josephine (2) 'I think she has lent it to P.'
LATER
Naomi (3)   'Well I'm hoping it's a girl really. If it's a boy it's wearing dresses.'
Josephine (2) 'If I have a girl next and Naomi has a boy…'
Naomi/
   Josephine   'We'll just swap.'
               Under 2 years

Few mothers are willing or able to pay for baby-sitting services. They doubted the safety of leaving children with teenage baby-sitters, other than older siblings, and preferred to rely on friends, baby-sitting circles, or family, such as aunts and uncles. Such services also rely on reciprocity, otherwise mothers feel guilty for making what they regard as unreasonable demands.

Judy (2)   'Well, we sort of do it together, we are friends and if Carmen has to go to the doctor I will look after her daughter, and if I have to go to the dentist or whatever, she looks after my son, or if it is after school we look after the older ones as well.'
Interviewer   'Do you feel guilty, though, asking people?'
Angela (2)   'Yes, you do.'

Judy	'But they don't make you feel guilty, you feel guilty.'
Liz (2)	'... like this morning. I had to be at play school at 11.30 and I have had to 'phone up the neighbours and ask them to pick P up with their daughter, and sort of keep her for half an hour, I feel as if I'm being cheeky sort of thing asking them to do it.'
Carmen (2)	[To Judy] 'It's like your sister's got our two today. You feel guilty don't you?'
	0 – 5 years

The presence of older children in the family can serve to increase family resources, as well as to put additional pressure on them. Older siblings bring significant economies of scale to the family budget. Mothers expect the capital equipment which they buy or are given on the birth of their first child to last for a subsequent child. In fact, a few mothers expressed guilt at the little which they had actually spent on a second child.

Jackie (2)	'Most of ours were gifts or passed on by relatives and we were thinking, we haven't bought anything, we felt awful.'
	6 – 10 years

Toys, books, games and clothes are also passed down, with some mothers, such as Naomi above, hoping for a second daughter in order to save money!

However, as children approach their teens, they become less willing to accept hand-ons and demand new, more expensive clothes and possessions.

Joyce (1)	'My C wouldn't be seen going anywhere near it [hand-on].'
Leslie (3)	'They don't mind wearing the odd thing that's handed on but when everything's handed-on it's depressing for them isn't it.'
Emma (1)	'Especially for girls I think 'cause they're at a difficult age.'
	11 – 16 years

As children get older still and begin to earn their own money, they begin to contribute to the 'cost' of their younger siblings. Mothers described relying on older brothers and sisters, not just for baby-sitting, but for providing treats and even purchasing clothes.

Steph (2)	'I think I find it easier with S because the next one up from S is 20, so all his brothers are now working, and a lot of the burden of his entertainment, his clothes, his shoes, and every-thing else, has been taken off me, because I tend to say to

him when he goes to his big brothers, "make sure you put your old trainers on please, he won't take you anywhere in them". Or, he's got a coat that he goes fishing in or just playing in, and it is really tatty … and I made him take that with him last time, so now he's got a new winter coat.'

6 – 16 years

It is apparent that, far from living in isolation, families continue to rely on networks of family and friends to enhance the size of the family budget, whether in cash or in kind. This suggests that attempts to force lone parents to have recourse to their own parents for support are misplaced – the extended family is already providing support, which for many poorer families is their only means of survival.

BUDGETING STRATEGIES

However successfully families maximise their resources, careful budgeting is required to ensure that needs can be met. In recent years, the failure of families to manage on low incomes has frequently been ascribed to their own inadequate budgeting strategies. It is suggested that if only families learnt to manage their money better through giving up smoking and drinking, buying fewer convenience foods and eating a healthier diet, they would not find themselves in such a parlous economic state.

The investigation of family budgeting strategies was not a central concern of this research. However, evidence from the group discussions suggests that most of these mothers already possessed a large, well-developed and sophisticated array of budgeting strategies which they deployed to ensure that family resources were used as economically as possible (see Chapter Ten). The particular strategy or strategies employed varies according to the budget area. We have chosen to concentrate here on clothing and food, but the mothers manage other budget areas with equal ingenuity. For example, second-hand purchases, although not acceptable for children's clothing, play a role in providing toys, books, games, and baby-equipment, such as prams, car seats and cots.

CLOTHES

Strategies for clothing children were numerous and sophisticated and varied little with socio-economic status. Presumably families on lower incomes impose the same strategies with greater rigidity on a smaller amount of money than their better-off colleagues.

We have already described the extensive use made of handed-on clothing. In addition, mothers had clear ideas about where and how to shop for new clothing and how that clothing should be used when purchased. Most mothers emphasised the need to buy the best quality clothes that you can afford. Buying the cheapest, from markets or 'cheap' discount shops, was seen as a false economy, especially when clothing can be passed on to younger siblings or 'sold on'.

June (2)   'For school clothes, school trousers, I buy good ones because they last longer. But I think it makes a difference if you've got somebody to pass them on to. If I spend £13 a pair on W's school trousers, I think they'll do G as well, and if I spend £9 a pair, they'll be worn out, and they won't do G as well, it's false economy really.'

Interviewer   'What about anybody else, do you buy for quality or cheapness?'

Selena (2)   'I always buy things that are going to last, but I sell my things anyway, so, if they've come to not fit one and I've got no one else they will fit, then I do sell them and buy something else.'
          6 – 16 years

However, there were exceptions to the 'buy quality' rule, especially among the mothers of young boys.

Adrienne (2)   'I do the opposite. I buy the cheap stuff ... because he's a little filthy tyke, in the garden, covered in mud, and he's on his knees, and it would break my heart if I'd spent a fortune. I buy him cheap jogging pants, and cheap T-shirts and let him do what he likes.'
          6 – 16 years

As well as 'buying quality' whenever possible, mothers also 'buy big', particularly, but not exclusively, in the case of expensive items such as winter coats.

Julie (3)   'I bought extra big last year so they fit them this year. The cheapest coat I've found for my boys was £25 for a winter coat and for them to last three or four months of that year, I think that's ridiculous. So I bought them extra big so they'd fit them this year.'

Kathy (3)   'Yeah, buy them too big and wear them, 'til they're too small.'
         6 – 10 years

Roz (1)   'What I do with mine is, I buy sweatshirt track-suit bottoms that are elasticated like these Reebok ones and are men's. And they are miles too long but they are great because they don't fall over his shoes … And jeans which are too long and fold up.'
         11 – 16 years

Sales of seasonal clothes are another useful source of cheap but high-quality clothing which, again, can be bought big and stored for the next season.

Lorraine (3)   'I try to buy them in the sales, you know, at the end of the summer and see if I can't get something for the following year in a bigger size to put by for them.'

Terry (3)   'I was going to buy my coats for Christmas but I said to P I'm not this year, I'm going after Christmas because they're all in the sales.'
         0 – 5 years

The use to which children's clothes are sometimes put can vary, thus hand-ons are used for after-school play clothes and new items kept for 'best'. Alternatively, clothing which was originally bought new changes its purpose as it gets older.

Selena (2)   'I tend to circulate mine, the best clothes go to the school clothes, and then they go to the playing out clothes, and then they have some new best clothes. I do it like that.'
         6 – 16 years

FOOD

Budgeting for food, in contrast, preoccupied only the lower income mothers. There was a sense that the idea of not being able to buy such food as you want, when you want it, did not occur to better-off mothers. They simply get in the car and drive to an out-of-town supermarket on a weekly basis. The experience of lower income mothers is somewhat different and they described a number of strategies for buying food.

The mothers choose the supermarkets carefully on the basis of a balance of price, quality and range of goods. Mothers try to shop around but lack of transport can be a severe problem, particularly for those on income support (IS).

Anita (3)   'I go to S because I can't walk anywhere else. I have to get a taxi back. I get my money on Monday from the post office and I get all my food in S and I get a taxi back because I can't carry it.'

    6 – 16 years

Mothers who live near supermarkets, shops and markets have an advantage. They described being able to shop towards the end of the day, when good bargains were to be had.

Vicky (3)   'I've found a way with that. If you go down [to the market] just before they pack up, they are giving the fruit away, they don't want to take it home with them, so they sell it cheap … It's the same with your bread in the supermarkets. If you go round the supermarkets when they are closing they are reducing the bread, and if you get that you can freeze it, you can get loaves for 25p.'

    6 – 16 years

Subtlety is required to ensure that, while buying for economy, children will actually eat what is provided.

Sally (2)   'If there's Frosties and then there's sugar-coated corn flakes, I buy the sugar-coated corn flakes.'
Ann (2)   'Well mine won't eat them, no.'
Sally (2)   'I usually buy one expensive one and keep the box and then fill it up.'
Ann (2)   'Ha! Sally!'
Sally (2)   'Well it makes them eat it. I'm sorry, but it does the trick! I mean, they still think it's Frosties.'

    6 – 10 years

However carefully mothers budget, it is advisable to have a fall-back position in case of emergencies, particularly when on IS.

Debbie (3)   'I always buy a sack of spuds to last me so I know I've always got something in.'

    0 – 5 years

These findings confirm those of a recent study of the food choices made by families on low incomes.[1] This showed that it was practically impossible for mothers on IS to 'ring-fence' money for food, however hard they tried. Food represented one of the few components of the budget which offered any degree of flexibility when unexpected bills arrived or other financial emergencies occurred. One of the main concerns of these mothers in providing food for the family was to avoid waste. Therefore, they bought what they knew their children would eat, since to attempt a radical change of diet would involve trial and error and, hence, waste. As a result, and somewhat ironically, their children often ate more of the foods they liked – fish fingers, beefburgers and so on – than their more affluent peers. Better-off parents can presumably afford waste, which providing a healthier, if less popular, diet for their children entails.

PARENTAL SACRIFICE

All parents make sacrifices, if only in the surrendering of privacy and independence. However, this book is concerned with the economic cost of parenting and it is apparent that, even in households with the most sophisticated budgeting strategies, and whatever the level of extra-household support, the level of economic sacrifice for children is high. Mothers frequently described situations in which they found themselves going without in order to ensure that their children had what they need or want.

Going without to provide 'needs' and 'wants' was an important distinction between mothers from different ends of the socio-economic spectrum. Better-off mothers described going without in order to provide 'wants' in terms of better opportunities for their children. In contrast, those on low incomes often find themselves making sacrifices so their children could get enough to eat.

Mandy (2)   'I have to say that my eldest daughter went on the school trip to Egypt, which I worked 70 odd hours a week, agency, as a nurse to pay for her to go 'cause I felt that was a wonderful opportunity.'
11 – 16 years

Roz (1)   'You know we sacrifice [to educate privately] it's not that we can afford to do this, we sacrifice to do this because we believe it's right. We make other, we go without a lot of things to be able to send him there and his brother will go there, but it is a sacrifice and I think the fact is I do feel

aggrieved because it's not that I'm thinking, "Oh, I want to send my child for the best academic education", I'm sending him because I believe spiritually it's the best thing for him.'
11 – 16 years

Anita (3)   'I cook for them and I don't have any.'
6 – 16 years

Roz and Anita highlight another important socio-economic distinction in the way in which mothers talk about parental sacrifice. Better-off mothers were less likely to be specific in describing the nature of the sacrifices made, simply saying they 'went without things'. Low-income mothers, in contrast, described a range of specific sacrifices of clothes and entertainment, as well as food.

June (3)   'I don't go out ... I haven't got any family here. I go out once a year – that's on my birthday for two hours when W's parents will look after the children for two hours.'
Under 5 years

Interviewer   'But you said that you will go without yourself?'
Lorraine (3)   'Oh yes, but I'm not that bothered. I mean I can live on cheese on toast and that doesn't bother me. But the kids have got to eat.'
Under 5 years

Val (3)   'If you need a coat and they need a coat...'
Various   'They get the coat first.'
Dawn (3)   'They get the coat and you get last year's.'
2 – 5 years

When it comes to clothing, however determined mothers are that their children should not wear second-hand, they do not apply the same rules to themselves. Many mothers are quite prepared to dress from charity shops and jumble sales and, as children get older, to wear their hand-ons.

Denise (3)   'It's got worse for me I would say. I have to wear my daughter's things, 'cause I can't afford to buy my own, I'm too busy trying to keep up with her, in competition ... I have her hand downs ... I've got her trousers that she's grown out of. I have pass downs from her, she always gets new and I get second-hand stuff.'
11 – 16 years

Interviewer	'Does anyone go to charity shops?'
June (2)	'We do don't we? Not for the children but for me.'
	11 – 16 years

Making sacrifices is seen as being as much a part of parenting as early-morning feeds and toilet training. Sacrifice is automatic and largely unquestioned. These two mothers are typical in that they sum up the unquestioned acceptance of putting children first, so that they will have every opportunity and the best possible childhood, often because of mothers' own bad experiences as children.

| *Sonia (2)* | 'I think you've got to give your kid a bit of money and a bit of enjoyment. As they get older they're going to scrimp and scrape and look after their own kids. You go without yourself to give to them don't you. I mean for Christmas I won't get anything, but she'll get what she wants.' |
| | *6 – 10 years* |

| *Joyce (1)* | 'My father used to say "I've booked the holiday", I mean I relate this to J and C time and time again, and on the Friday night he'd come home and say "we're not going on holiday tomorrow, we can't afford it", you know, and I can't think of anything worse than being told the day before you go that you can't go and I think that's probably why we have our holidays and we do things for the children because that is ... I mean I wasn't deprived, I was loved, but things like that stick in your mind.' |
| | *11 – 16 years* |

CONCLUSION

In this chapter we have tried to show the myriad mechanisms by which parents attempt to cope with the economic pressures of child rearing. Mothers possess a plethora of strategies for maximising household resources and stretching them as far as possible. Whatever the size of the family budget, children come first in all things, with parents on low incomes prepared to sacrifice their own well-being to a remarkable extent.

The degree to which all families continue to rely on the wider family and friends for support was surprising. This suggests that any attempts to force lone parents to have recourse to their own parents for assistance would be fruitless. For many such parents the wider family is already filling the gap between benefit levels and an income on which they can survive.

NOTES

1. B Dobson, A Beardsworth, T Keil and R Walker, *Diet, Choice and Poverty*, Family Policy Studies Centre, 1994.

10 How mothers use child benefit

Robert Walker, Sue Middleton
and Michelle Thomas

As a very explicit statement of the commitment of successive governments to assisting with the costs of child rearing, child benefit, its future and even its abolition, has remained at the centre of political debates. Key questions which have been raised include whether families spend child benefit on the children and whether it makes a real difference to the well-being of the family.

Also, as a fixed sum of money for each child, child benefit provides a particularly useful avenue for exploring the different ways in which mothers actually employ the budgeting strategies described in Chapter Nine.

It has been about ten years since research was last undertaken to determine the uses to which mothers put child benefit.[1] At that time, it seemed to be spent largely on children's food, clothing and shoes, and also on school expenses, pocket money and general household spending. Mothers believed the benefit to be essential in providing for the needs of their children and deeply appreciated the fact that it was a regular, reliable and direct payment.

In the intervening period the real incomes of families in work have risen noticeably, while the value of child benefit has fallen in relation to prices, even allowing for the fact that it has been restructured to pay more cash for a first child. As a result, some commentators have argued that child benefit may be less needed, especially by better-off families.

In the six orientation groups (see Appendix) we took time therefore to explore and update our understanding of the ways in which child benefit is used. This was supplemented by two groups sponsored by the Department of Social Security (DSS), in which the topic was investigated in more depth.[2] One of the latter groups involved mothers drawn from socio-economic categories D and E, the other mothers in categories A and B.[3]

MANAGING AND PLANNING EXPENDITURES

As noted in the Introduction, it was mothers who assumed day-to-day responsibility for spending on children, irrespective of the budgeting model adopted by families. Among other things, this responsibility entails the ability to manage the demands of children and to plan spending so as to provide the things that mothers determine (or agree that) their children require. Planning involves recognising when large demands are likely to fall (the beginning of the school year, winter, Christmas and school trips in the summer); ensuring that sufficient cash is at hand to meet the daily demands; and finally, perhaps most difficult of all, budgeting for the unexpected.

Lorraine (3)   'Summer is very easy, it's the winter that's difficult. Summer you can kit them out very cheaply with T-shirts and things off the market, a pair of sandals or trainers. Winter comes, they've got to have jackets and tights. They go to school and get through tights at about two pairs a week ... They've got to have school shoes, they've got to have trainers, hat, gloves, scarves.'

      0 – 5 years

As already described in Chapter Nine, planning involves a knowledge of what is available, where, and at what price. The search for economy, for bargains and for ways to reduce costs is apparent right across the range of incomes embraced by the groups.

Successful planning can ease the problems of managing children's demands. Child benefit is often an important instrument in mothers' financial planning.

Wendy (3)   'I had to kit her out completely for school for winter, coat, shoes, boots, leggings, the lot! And that was just one child! So that £104 [child benefit] just paid for the one child to be kitted out for winter ... That was not going stupid and going to expensive shops. That was literally shopping all day in Leicester looking for the best bargains for the money.'

      Child benefit group, any age

FINANCIAL TOOL

Indeed, listening to mothers talking in the groups, it became apparent that they explicitly use child benefit as a device or tool to help them manage their family budgets. As with any tool, child benefit has particular characteristics which govern its use and make it more valuable in some circumstances than others.

The women we spoke to would probably recognise five features of child benefit that determine its use:

- it is paid as an identifiable entity;
- it comes in a lump sum and is cumulative;
- it is regular and dependable;
- it is generally paid to mothers;
- it is intended for the children.

The fact that it is identifiable means that it can be kept separate, either to be used for a particular purpose or to act as a 'safe' to protect some money from incessant demands, perhaps to serve as a short- or longer-term safety net for the family. Very few of the mothers had their child benefit paid by automatic credit transfer, one reason given for this was to avoid it becoming 'lost' in a joint account, or in the general household expenditure.

The financial demands made by children are often 'lumpy' (requests for large sums at irregular intervals). Child benefit is paid in a similar way and is consequently seen as an almost perfect antidote to the pair of worn out shoes.

Jenny (3)	'The good thing is it comes in one lump sum, that's why it's normally spent on a big item...'
Wendy (3)	'Yeah.'
Jackie (3)	'Say, like, you've got a fiver a week spare out your wages; you don't save that fiver ... where the child benefit comes in one lump sum.'
Maureen (3)	'You can't touch it until that date.'
	Child benefit group, any age

Because it is paid regularly, child benefit enables mothers to plan ahead in the knowledge that, if need be, they can spend now and be sure that they will have cash to cope with some unforeseen contingency in the weeks ahead. Alternatively, they might decide to allocate it for some anticipated future expense without fear of spending it beforehand.

Wendy (3)   'Mine's planned out before I get to it.'

Jackie (3)   'Yeah. You spend it before you draw it out, don't ya, yeah.'

Wendy (3)   'That's right, mentally I've worked out what I've got to get out of it for the children and I basically know what's left, which isn't very much when there's three of them. But, like, it's due 1st of November, I basically know what I've got to get with it already.'

              Child benefit group, any age

Because it is paid directly to them, mothers have complete control over how it is spent. It may be their only source of financial autonomy and, at times of crisis, represents a valuable safety net.

Lastly, child benefit is often seen as having a specific purpose – it is for the children – even although it is paid to the mother. This gives it a special status, a further reason (or helpful excuse) to protect it or to spend it wisely. For some, the name was a directive as to how the benefit should be spent. Moreover, although spending child benefit on the family could be presented as indirectly benefiting children, many of the mothers felt a little guilty if they did not spend it directly on their offspring, even if they believed that they had no other choice.

Linda (1)   'I suppose it's because we get it for a purpose and it's child benefit so you like to think that that's what you're actually doing with it.'

              Child benefit group, any age

With these five characteristics in mind, the mothers in the groups described at least seven ways in which they used their child benefit. Key differences were the extent to which it was spent directly on children, and the time period for which it was saved. The various uses were apparent in all the groups, but the precise circumstances differed both in the mothers' intent and in the outcome. The groups, it will be recalled, were selected so as to differ in terms of respondents' social and marital status and the age of children. All these factors were probably important in determining the precise ways in which the benefit was used.

GENERAL HOUSEKEEPING

Although by no means the commonest use of child benefit, some mothers simply merged it into their household budget. These mothers appear to be concentrated among respondents with the highest and lowest incomes.

For those on the highest incomes (typically in the AB groups), child benefit would simply have been part of the income paid directly into the current account, to be drawn on as needed. Being a small amount in relation to their overall spending, it was sometimes not really noticed. Occasionally, the account is in joint names but child benefit is mostly paid into a separate account used by the woman. Often mothers said that they made no distinctions at all between family members but, since their accounts were mostly used for day-to-day housekeeping, a considerable, though unknown, proportion of the benefit must have been spent on the children. Indeed, even among families with high incomes, some mothers saw it as being 'needed' for their daily expenditure on food.

Jackie (1)   'I get mine paid into the bank and sometimes I wish I didn't because I don't notice it's there so...'

                0 – 5 years

Jane (1)   'What's a budget?'

Diane (1)   'Where you do everything on direct debit so you don't spend it! That's how we budget.'

Jane (1)   'I budget by going to the bank towards the end of the month and checking how much money's left in the account! "Oh God, we can't eat for a week and a half!"'

                Child benefit group, any age

Some of the mothers in the high-income groups who simply added child benefit to their housekeeping felt the need to justify this strategy. The benefit was paid for children and that is mostly where it went.

Janet (1)   'Am I denying the children something by not earmarking the £70 specifically for them? I've just started to wonder for the first time. And I don't think I am, because it [child benefit] is such a small amount compared with the amount that they cost as part of the family. Just in terms of the general running costs.'

                Child benefit group, any age

This concern about the proper use of child benefit was echoed among the less affluent women, who felt themselves forced into the position of using the benefit for basic household necessities.

Pat (3)   'It's called child benefit, but I pay the gas with mine but really I should be spending it on the kids really shouldn't I?'

Lorraine (3)   'Yeah. But what can you get.'

| Debbie (3) | 'You can't really afford to, can you?' |
| | 0 – 5 years |

Jackie (3)	'I don't spend that full £40 just on like things for Alice. I mean it does go on food as well, 'cos she is eating food.'
Roz (3)	'Oh no.'
Maureen (3)	'Mine helps out with bills sometimes.'
Janet (3)	'…but they don't need everything, do they?'
Jenny (3)	'Which you've got to, because, you've got to have electric.'
	Child benefit group, any age

As the mothers they felt they had no alternative, however, such a concern was secondary. This was especially true of lone parents on income support (IS). Child benefit was necessary to tide them over from one week to the next. Indeed, most lone parents were grateful to be able to pick up the benefit weekly, because that was the only way that they could eke out their IS. They needed the maximum flexibility to match resources to needs and could not afford to 'ring-fence' any element, however small.

Interviewer	'But the rest of you collect it weekly?'
Sandy (3)	'Yes, it's needed weekly.'
Vicky (3)	'It helps you through the week.'
Anita (3)	'You get to Sunday night and you've got a child that's hungry.'
Vicky (3)	'Yes, that's right.'
Interviewer	'So what do you spend it on?'
Sue (3)	'It just goes on normal household expenses. I don't think you can put it by, and say that it is solely for my children, it just isn't possible.'
Anita (3)	'Especially if you're on income support, because on income support you cannot afford to live, I'm going to pay my electricity bill, or my gas bill.'
Vicky (3)	'They just give you enough to survive on, we get our money on a Monday, and we save the family allowance until the end of the week, so we've got enough for the weekend for a Sunday meal, otherwise we wouldn't survive on the bit we get. You don't get any extras for presents or shoes…'
	6 – 16 years

USE FOR A SPECIFIC PURPOSE

Quite a large number of mothers who did not deliberately save their child benefit nevertheless kept it separate to pay particular expenses. Sometimes they set it aside for spending on the children, other women use it to meet general expenses. This latter strategy again seemed to be fairly common among less well-off households but was not restricted to them. Some mothers use child benefit to pay regular bills, such as the electricity and gas, others set it aside for clothing.

Lorraine (3)   'I draw my income support each week to live on and then I use the other [child benefit] to pay for the bills. I keep that in the bank ... The amount I get on income support I spend every week, I don't have any money to put away for any bills or anything so I use that [child benefit] for bills.'
0 – 5 years

Yet others use it for little luxuries and treats for the family and sometimes for themselves.

Jackie (1)   'Haircut for me. When I first got it I thought what am I going to do with this money? I thought that the best thing to do is to keep that money for me and I usually spend it on me. I have my hair cut.'
0 – 5 years

Keeping the child benefit aside for the children seemed a fairly common practice and has similarities to the practice of those who deliberately save it for their children. Again, the distinction may be between those who have the capacity to defer consumption and those who do not. The benefit was most frequently spent on children's clothing, especially shoes and kit for school.

Maureen (3)   'At the moment it's sitting in my purse in a separate compartment. On Saturday I am going to kit them all [the children] out.'
Child benefit group, any age

Mothers also often used the benefit to buy disposable nappies. This was perceived as either essential or as a treat for the mother. Other purchases, more frequently mentioned in the higher status groups, included books, tuition, toys and treats.

There is some evidence that mothers of older children interpret the meaning of child benefit literally. They hand it over to the child, on the understanding that the child then takes responsibility for paying for certain goods and services. This is seen as having the twin advantages of limiting mothers' own spending and passing on financial management skills.

Felicity (3)   'I found as well that over the years, well I would say the last two years, the money that they need was horrendous, and I said, well, I'm not having this, so what I started to do was I used to get the family allowance and I used to, well, I give 'em £8 each pocket money a week, and I said you manage it yourself, you take yourself to the pictures, you, obviously I'll buy the clothes. I mean I wouldn't expect them to buy that. But anything they need they had to spend and manage themselves on £8. And they felt great because they'd got it in a lump sum and yet they were managing that.'
11 – 16 years

Although mothers could see the advantages of this strategy, the realities of the family's financial circumstances intervene to prevent its implementation.

Jo (2)   'It's too much of a sum for the family budget to give up unfortunately.'
Alison (2)   'They do start asking for family allowance, my daughter started asking for it.'
Chris (1)   'You know we'd already talked about it when they were young, we decided "when our children are 13 we're going to give them the family allowance..." then the recession happened.'
Chorus   'That's right. Yeah.'
Chris (1)   'Nice idea, pity about the reality.'
11 – 16 years

A few families with younger children used their child benefit to cover the costs of childcare, although there was comment as to whether the beneficiary of this expenditure was the child or the mother. In one of the AB groups, however, mothers argued cogently that nursery education should be a right enjoyed by all parents and cited the situation in other countries to support their case.

Setting money aside was seen by some people to be a 'luxury' (even among the AB groups) in that in their households child benefit was just absorbed into daily living.

Janet (1)   'I think it would be a luxury to be able to separate it. At the moment the children are so much part of the household, they eat the food, they use the electricity, the hot water and everything, virtually. I mean, there must be very few categories that are solely for them and it's almost like their contribution to the household expenses.'

Child benefit group, any age

PUTTING CHILD BENEFIT TO ONE SIDE

Some mothers kept their child benefit to one side, not so much to spend on their children or particular items, but to ensure that they had enough money to see them through a particular lean period (the couple of days to the next IS Giro, or longer). In the case of one better-off household, the benefit was paid into an account and used as the 'family safety net' to be drawn on at the end of the month. Another AB mother used her child benefit to meet the family food bill in the last week of every month.

Jane (1)   'Child benefit's paid into that account to hide it from ourselves, basically. We tend to spend until we have slightly overdrawn our joint account. And therefore if we hide money from ourselves in the building society, we can use it to bail ourselves out.'

Child benefit group, any age

SHORT-TERM SAVING

Quite a large number of mothers consciously saved their child benefit for specific purchases. The difference between these women and those mentioned earlier is that they tended not spend it each time it came due. The distinction is a fine one, in that some mothers felt that their child benefit was accumulating from one month to the next and were grateful that they could not draw it out until it was due.

Sharon (3)   'Well, mine mainly goes on shoes, because I get mine once a month, and she can only have the Clarks shoes, because her feet are too wide, and they are £25, £26 a pair.'

6 – 16 years

The items for which mothers save their child benefit were wide-ranging but, in most cases, it seems that it was saved for the child.

This may be because saving is a very deliberate act and mothers are confronted with the name 'child benefit' and what they assume to be its purpose. Children's clothes again topped their lists, but things like children's parties, Christmas and big toys were also mentioned.

Steph (2) 'You leave it a fortnight, you can get a pair of shoes and a pair of jeans out of it. If you don't leave it a fortnight, I do occasionally spend it, but it's never on me, it's always on something that they need, or they want, or a birthday. If there is a birthday coming up, I tend to leave it in as long as I can, so that I can pay for a boring meal at McDonalds or something with his friends.'

6 – 16 years

Jackie (3) 'At least when it's in a separate book and you go and collect it once a month, you've got the money in your hand you know it's for the children. If it got direct debit into the bank there it would be with all the other things.'

Child benefit group, any age

The attractions of child benefit for savers, and for those who set it aside, is that it is paid as a labelled entity which comes directly to mothers and, if collected from the post office, is protected by the need to make a journey. This final point is an important attraction of payment through post offices and may limit the use of automatic credit transfer.

Alice (2) 'I used to have mine paid directly into the bank and I found that you didn't notice it. It just went in with the money and I found that friends of mine would have it paid at the post office ... So I had it altered when my daughter was born. I had it at the post office and I find I can use it far more specifically for the children.'

0 – 5 years

LONG-TERM SAVING

A few mothers managed to accumulate their child benefit over a long period and others, especially those with very small children, had aspirations to do so. Perhaps not surprisingly, long-term saving was most frequent among the higher income groups, although even here it was the exception rather than the rule. Occasionally, the saving was for a specific purpose, more often it was a general purpose account for the children. In one case child benefit was used to help fund family holidays.

Carmen (2)	'My idea was to save everything and put it in a bank and keep it for her when she grew older.'
Sally (2)	'Yes, that is what we tried to do actually, but I don't know whether it will work. We have opened a building society account.'
Carmen (2)	'It does work to a certain degree but then when she does need shoes and we don't have the cash...'
Sally (2)	'You go dipping into it.'
Carmen (2)	'Yes. You start dipping into it.'

0 – 5 years

LAPSED SAVERS

However much some mothers wanted to save up their child benefit, and despite the safeguards of the post office or hiding it in a special compartment in their purse, they found that they were forced to spend it. The above quotation, which reflects doubts about the mothers' ability not 'to dip into' their child benefit, was taken from one of the C1C2 groups, but the pressures appeared much greater among the two-parent families in the DE groups. Most lone parents did not even try to save it.

Jenny (3)	'I've gotta try and save mine 'cos, there's two [payments] now before Christmas, isn't there, if you have it monthly? And I'm trying to save it towards Christmas.'
Wendy (3)	'Mmm, that's what mine's for, yeah...'
Roz (3)	'What do you do for nappies then when you're saving it? If you don't mind me asking that...'
Jackie (3)	'Rob Peter to pay Paul...'
Janet (3)	'I'm like that sometimes. I think right I'm not gonna draw it, I'm gonna try not to draw it out this month so that I can save it. But it gets to about a week after it was due and I think, "no I need it".'
Maureen (3)	'I've never managed to do that.'
Roz (3)	'No I've not.'
Jenny (3)	'I've not yet but I'm determined. I've got to otherwise...'

Child benefit group, any age

FRITTERING IT AWAY

A few mothers admitted to frittering away their child benefit and others sought devices to prevent themselves from doing this. Nevertheless, the purchases made, such as additional clothes for their children, were not always ones that would universally be considered as 'frittering away' their money. However, one middle-class family did pay child benefit into an account which they then forgot about for a number of years. On 'discovering' the account, they spent some of the money, leaving the rest to pay for the university education of their son.

Ann (2) 'Food or a Saturday night out. If it is in my purse I spend it, I am terrible, I couldn't do what you do and save it up.'
     0 – 5 years

Jenny (3) 'You've got it [child benefit] in your pocket, you nip in Adams or you get a new dress or a new T-shirt they don't need. But you've got this money, and say, "oh well, that's nice!" So I probably would be tempted to have it.'
     Child benefit group, any age

Janet (3) 'No, I just have it, like I say I have it and I go and draw it out and it stays in my purse for if Paul needs anything, but sometimes when the money from the bank that I've got in my purse has gone and like we're not going to the bank machine, or you know, I can't get to the bank, then it gets borrowed out of the family allowance and it goes, it disappears, the £40 I get a month disappears on some…'
     Child benefit group, any age

REFLECTIONS

It is unlikely that these are the only seven ways of using child benefit, or that mothers stick to one use. From force of circumstance, or reasons of choice, women may move from one mode of budgeting to another, or may practice more than one kind contemporaneously. Moreover, some women find it very difficult to save child benefit, whatever their intentions. Likewise, they may wish to set it aside for the children but have to raid it to pay a pressing bill. Also, because expenditures on children are inherently 'lumpy', mothers may not need to spend it exclusively on children all the time, in which case it may get absorbed into the general household budget for a period.

While the uses identified may be indicative, rather than definitive, they are largely consistent with those reported in earlier studies. Hedges and Hyatt, for example, noted that most parents saw child benefit as a form of support for families which should be used for the benefit of the children, not as money always to be applied directly and exclusively to children's needs.[4] A favourite use of child benefit was for children's shoes, clothing and similar periodic expenses but, when resources were tight, it would be used to meet the most pressing need.

Therefore, while the real value of child benefit may not have kept up with inflation, there is no evidence that mothers have changed the way in which they use it. Nor does recent evidence suggest that child benefit is any less valued.[5] Instead, it is clear that the women in the groups mostly saw child benefit as a tool for domestic financial management with particular characteristics that make it especially useful: it is paid to the mother on behalf of children and comes as a regular, lump sum that is clearly identifiable.

NOTES

1. A Hedges and J Hyatt, *Attitudes of Beneficiaries to Child Benefit and Benefits for Young People*, Social and Community Planning Research (SCPR), 1985. A Walsh and R Lister, *Mother's Lifeline*, Child Poverty Action Group, 1985.
2. A further report of the findings of this research is contained in R Walker, S Middleton and M Thomas, *Mostly on the Children: the significance of child benefit in family budgets*, Centre for Research in Social Policy, Working Paper 218, 1993.
3. Since the age of children was not specified for recruitment of these groups, the age identifier following each verbatim quotation has been replaced with 'Child benefit group, any age'.
4. Hedges and Hyatt, *op cit.*
5. R Walker, S Middleton and M Thomas, 'Mothers' attachment to child benefit', *Benefits*, Issue 11, Autumn 1994. J Bradshaw and C Stimson, *Use and Contribution of Child Benefit within the Family Budget*, Department of Social Policy and Social Work, University of York (forthcoming).

Conclusion: the reality of childhood poverty in Britain

Sue Middleton and Robert Walker

The main theme of this book has been the emphasis which both parents and children place on 'participation': the right of every child to share in the activities, experiences and lifestyle of the community in which s/he is born and brought up. In a materialistic world, the ability of a child to participate is predicated to a large extent on access to goods, services and activities, all of which have a financial cost.

So what is the minimum financial cost to parents to ensure that their child's participation can be secured? Chapter One describes the minimum essential budgets for children in four age groups. These budgets were drawn up and agreed by parents from different parts of the country and from all socio-economic backgrounds. They believed their budgets represented the minimum which any child in Britain in the 1990s needs to ensure that s/he has the opportunity to 'fit in' with her/his peers and, hence, to grow up into law-abiding, useful citizens. These budgets could not be described as extravagant: parents included no allowance for video machines, computers or eating out. Indeed, none of the parents, including those on low incomes or income support (IS), would have found their minimum budgets acceptable for their own children. However, the results suggest that large numbers of British children are growing up in families which have far less money to allocate to their children than the minimum recommended by parents. IS levels for dependent children would need to be increased by amounts varying from £3.01 per week (11 per cent) for 11- to 16-year-old girls, to £11.57 per week (56 per cent) for two- to five-year-old boys, if the parents' minimum budget standards were to be met. It is worth reiterating that these figures were not produced by researchers. They represent the considered and agreed views of the people who are actually doing the job of bringing up children and who are, arguably, best placed to judge children's financial needs.

Chapters Two and Three described what children have and do and what they feel they need in order to participate in the world around them. The similarities in the aspirations and patterns of ownership of children from different socio-economic backgrounds suggest that they now share a common culture of acquisition which has major implications for the ability of poorer families to meet the consumption aspirations of their children. Chapter Three provides the first indication of another recurring theme in the book: that children from less affluent families are taught to limit their aspirations at an early age. It is clear that, whilst there are only marginal differences between the things which richer and poorer children do on a day-to-day basis, their opportunities to gain from the experience of visiting other parts of Britain, much less other countries, vary markedly. More disturbing is the finding that the less affluent children to whom we listened had already limited their aspirations to travel and see the world.

In drawing up the minimum budgets in Chapter One, parents were conscious of the pressures experienced by their own children which translate into financial demands on the family budget. Chapters Four, Five and Six describe three sources of such pressure on children: friends, particularly in relation to clothes; school; and advertising. The picture which emerges is one of intense pressure on children to have and do things if they are not to be socially and, perhaps of more concern, educationally excluded. The financial costs of all aspects of school, described in Chapter Five, in turn bring particular pressure on parents. They are only too aware of the importance of educational success to their children's future, as well as of the misery which results from social exclusion at school and elsewhere for children who can be identified by their peers as different because of their poverty.

The pressure on children to conform to peer group norms seems particularly intense in relation to clothing. In Chapter Four children described witnessing both verbal and physical abuse of other children in their school who were deemed by their peers to be dressed inappropriately. On a more encouraging note, it does seem that the pressure to acquire expensive, designer label clothes begins to decline as children reach maturity and financial independence. However, this will be of small comfort to parents of younger children who have seen the consequences of wearing the 'wrong' make of training shoes.

The all-pervasive nature of advertising in modern society is the source of many of the judgements which children make about what they and their peers must have in order to avoid such social exclusion. Chapter Six showed the extent to which advertising, in particular on television, has become a recognised part of many children's lives by the age of seven. Despite the reassuring cynicism displayed by some children about the motivations of advertisers and the accuracy of their claims, it is clear that advertising does have an effect on children. This is sometimes in the direct sense of making children want the advertised item, but more often by making them aware of the new products whose desirability they can investigate.

The combination of school, peer and advertising pressures is inevitably translated by children into financial demands on their parents and/or other family members. As Chapter Seven shows, children's strategies for persuading, even coercing, parents and others to meet these demands are multifarious and often very sophisticated. For example, children are only too well aware of the priority which parents give to educational expenditure and are prepared to exploit the 'I need it for school' argument whenever possible. However, there is some indication that children from less affluent families differ in the persuasion strategies they adopt, being more likely to report direct action – door-banging and so on – than their wealthier peers. These are the very strategies which they admit are likely to be least successful and their continued use may simply reflect the more frequent frustration of their demands experienced by poorer children.

Chapter Eight has described the strategies which parents, in turn, employ to resist their children's demands. After all, whatever the size of the family budget and however successfully it is manipulated, there comes a point where children's demands have to be limited, either from financial necessity or because it is thought to be wrong continually to give children everything they ask for. In these situations parents can either say 'no' and stick to it, or reach a compromise with their children. While such compromises eventually involve giving in, either partially or completely, mothers believe that they are invaluable to children since this is the process by which mothers pass on their sophisticated budgeting strategies to the next generation. In this, poorer children are doubly disadvantaged. First, their parents are forced to say 'no' more frequently to more requests but with less consistency because of the week-to-week uncertainties of the family finances. Financial discipline is exerted out of necessity, rather than any decision about what it is good or bad for the child to have or do. What cannot be afforded one week may be possible the next. The rationale for such apparent inconsistency must escape many children, particularly the younger ones, who will find it difficult to understand why they were allowed that expensive ice cream last week but are denied a packet of crisps this week. The feelings of frustration which result may provide at least part of the explanation for the increased level of door-banging and tantrums among poorer children suggested by Chapter Seven. Second, poorer children lose out because their parents cannot afford risking waste involved in giving children the financial autonomy necessary to practice budgeting strategies.

However, saying 'no' is just one of the weapons in the parents' armoury for coping with financial pressure from their children. Most parents have sophisticated strategies for managing the family budget, such strategies being particularly highly developed among the poorer ones. First, they will use all available means to expand their total budget. Contrary to conventional wisdom, it is apparent that for many less well-off parents, the financial support of other family members and friends remains a crucial element in their lives. They provide extra money in crises and are also regular sources of handed-on clothing, holidays and other treats, and free childcare.

Second, parents deploy strategies to ensure that available resources are used as economically as possible. The methods used by mothers to guarantee that their children are adequately fed and clothed suggest that, far from wasting money, all mothers – but the less well-off in particular – perform miracles of budgetary management on an almost daily basis.

Third, all parents make financial sacrifices for their children but, among the mothers to whom we listened, crucial differences again emerged between those from different ends of the socio-economic spectrum. Better-off mothers described going without in order to meet their children's 'wants', in terms of providing them with better opportunities. In contrast, poorer mothers make sacrifices to meet their children's 'needs', frequently describing situations where they went without themselves to ensure that their children had enough to eat.

The sophistication of mothers' budgetary strategies emerged in even greater detail from our examination of the uses to which mothers put child benefit. We identified at least seven ways in which mothers use the benefit and it is unlikely that these are the only uses, or that mothers stick to one use. From force of circumstances, or reasons of choice, women may move from one use to another, or put child benefit to more than one use at a time. However mothers chose to use it, and although its real value may not have kept up with inflation, child benefit remains a highly valued tool for domestic financial management. Women find it particularly useful because it is a regular lump sum paid to them on behalf of their children.

A disturbing gap emerged in our work between poorer parents' perceptions of their children's reactions to living on a low income and the attitudes and aspirations of the less affluent children who took part in the research. Poorer parents attempt to teach their children about the limitations of the family budget from an early age. They believe that their children learn not to ask for things and, because of this, that they genuinely understand and accept that they cannot have and do the same things as their wealthier peers. However, this is clearly only half the story. Children say that, while they limit their aspirations to travel and, as they get older, their demands on parents when they know money is particularly tight, they continue to want the same things, whatever the financial circumstances of their families. Indeed, Chapter Seven has suggested that children from less affluent families continue to shout and bang doors when attempting to get what they want. Further research is planned to try and explain this apparent discrepancy between the perceptions of children and parents. What is clear, however, is that many poorer children experience daily frustration of their economic aspirations.

It may be that in this gap between parents and children lies an indication of the reality of childhood poverty in 1990s Britain. The determination that children should be able to 'participate' and its negative corollary, the fear of exclusion, are of equal importance to parents and children alike. Yet it is equally apparent that many parents must be unable to meet the financial demands which 'participation' involves, however skilfully they juggle resources or however great their own sacrifices. Their children begin to experience the reality of their 'differentness' at an early age. Parents try to teach them not to ask, and the children begin to learn how to go without.

Much effort has been expended in recent months and years on attempts to prove or disprove the continued existence of poverty among children in Britain, and ensuing quantification of the numbers who can be defined as 'poor' or 'relatively deprived'. Such debates have sometimes seemed to take place on the same intellectual plane, and to be equally as sterile, as theological debates about whether, and how many, angels can fit on a pinhead. To continue the analogy we would suggest that the answer is only of importance to the angel who wants to get onto the pinhead and cannot find room to stand. Equally, for the children and parents living on a low income it matters little whether they are called 'poor' or 'relatively deprived'. What matters to them is that they are excluded from full participation in the world around them. They are denied access to the same material possessions and opportunities as their friends. We would suggest that it is in their experience of that exclusion that the reality of childhood poverty can be most usefully, and sadly, discovered.

METHODS USED IN THE STUDY

LISTENING TO PARENTS

The experiences of parents described in this book are the result of a total of 24 group discussions which were held with parents between September 1993 and February 1994. The participants were professionally recruited and a short questionnaire was administered at recruitment to establish household composition, employment status, housing tenure and size, possession of a range of consumer durables and household income.

PARENTS AND EXPENDITURES ON CHILDREN

For the purposes of these group discussions, recruiters were asked to recruit parents 'who had the major responsibility for day-to-day expenditures on children'. In the event, all the participants were mothers. Parents were asked to concentrate on one of their children within the given age range of the group for which they had been recruited. The groups were also balanced in terms of the sex of the children under discussion. Nine participants were recruited for each group to try and ensure an attendance of eight and, from a total of 198 recruited, 193 mothers actually participated in the group discussions.

The groups took place in three stages. First, six 'orientation' groups were held in September 1993 with the aim of ensuring that the ideas and concepts employed in later stages of the project would be informed and understood by parents. All six groups took place in the Midlands, three in a city and three in a small market town in order to highlight any differences in the experiences of parents having differential access to shops, markets and other facilities. Two of the groups were made up of parents from socio-economic groups A and B (professional and managerial), two groups from socio-economic groups C1 and C2 (other non-manual and skilled manual workers), and two from socio-economic groups D and E (semi- and unskilled workers and income support recipients). Socio-economic status was determined on the basis of the occupation of the main earner. Three of the groups were made up of mothers who all had at least one child under the age of six years, the other three groups all having at least one child between the ages of six and 16.

Nine categories of possible expenditure on children were identified prior to these groups and a topic guide was drawn up for each category. The categories were: Food; Clothes; Activities; Possessions; Children's 'own' money, including pocket money, savings, earnings, etc; Fuel; Housing; Baby Equipment; and Other Goods and Services, such as laundry, toiletries and transport. As it was not possible for each group to discuss every expenditure category, selected categories were covered by different groups.

In the groups, parents were asked to compile lists of items which their children had in the expenditure categories allocated to their group. The difficulties of producing each list were then discussed, as well as other relevant issues contained in the topic guide, such as family budgeting patterns, shopping, other sources of items, pressures on parents and children.

The second phase of 12 groups, which took place in December 1993 and January 1994, had the dual aims of testing instrumentation for the proposed national survey and producing an agreed minimum budget standard for children of varying ages. Four groups were held in each of three locations: a large city in the north of England; a smaller city in the Midlands; a rural area in the south of England. Each of these groups were socio-economically mixed, with roughly equal numbers of mothers from socio-economic groups A and B; C1 and C2; and D and E. The groups were divided into four age groups of children, as follows: two of the groups included mothers who all had at least one child under two; three groups with at least one child aged over two and under six years; three groups with at least one child aged over six but under 11 years; and four groups with at least one child over 11 years but under 17 years of age.

For one week prior to the group discussion each mother completed a set of instrumentation on the particular budget areas which were to be discussed in the group. A detailed description of the methods used in these groups to produce the budget standard is included in Chapter One.

The third and final set of four groups was held in the same Midlands city in February. The aim of these groups was to check the lists of minimum essential requirements for children of different ages produced by the previous 12 groups and to reach a final consensus from which budget standards could be derived. Each of these groups was, again, socio-economically mixed and one group was recruited for each of the four age groups. A description of the content of these groups can also be found in Chapter One.

PARENTS AND CHILD BENEFIT

The two groups which discussed child benefit exclusively took place in a large Midlands city. Only mothers were recruited, since it is to the mother that child benefit is paid. One of the groups was made up of mothers from socio-economic groups A and B, and the other from socio-economic groups D and E. No restrictions were placed on the recruiters in terms of numbers or age of children in the family. Three of the total of 18 mothers were single parents mainly in the DE group.

All of the 24 group discussions were recorded and the tapes transcribed. The transcripts were then systematically analysed, using a mixture of computer-aided and manual techniques based mainly on derivatives of cognitive or semantic mapping and thematic indexing. Reference to the original source of the information was retained so that it was possible to analyse the material by respondent, age group of child, socio-economic status, and region. Throughout this book our aim has been to allow parents to speak for themselves as far as possible and editing of quotations has therefore been kept to a minimum. The names of mothers have been changed to protect their anonymity. Where a group facilitator has been quoted, her/his comments are prefixed with 'Interviewer'.

Each verbatim quotation includes the 'name' of the mother, the socio-economic group of the mother and the age group of children being discussed by the group.

LISTENING TO CHILDREN

The children who took part in this research came from four schools: a primary and secondary school in the north of England; and a primary and secondary school in the Midlands. Since it was not possible to question the children about family income, the schools were chosen in order to explore any differences which might emerge between children from different socio-economic backgrounds. Therefore, the northern secondary school had a large percentage (over 80 per cent) of children living in privately owned housing (described for convenience throughout the book as 'more affluent'), whereas the primary school had a large percentage of children living in fairly run-down local authority owned housing (described as 'less affluent'). The catchment area 'status' was reversed for the Midlands schools. Children were asked about the occupation of the adults with whom they lived, and examination of their responses suggests that the choice of schools successfully discriminated between children from different socio-economic backgrounds.

The children came from four school year groups, corresponding approximately to the ages of eight, 11, 13 and 16 years, and all the research took place in school. Letters were sent to parents allowing them to opt their children out of the research but very few did so. Children themselves were allowed to opt out in the secondary schools if they wished, but only two did so, in the northern secondary school.

The wide discrepancy in age and ability of the children required the use of a range of interviewing techniques. In the primary schools 12 children were selected by class teachers from each of school years three and six and interviewed in four groups of three. Teachers were asked to select the groups on the basis of friendship patterns and to avoid mixing boys and girls in the groups wherever possible, in order to help the children feel comfortable. In the event, all four of the groups in the northern primary school turned out to be mixed in order to maintain friendship groups. Three sessions were held with each of the groups, each of which followed a similar pattern: the first 30 minutes were devoted to semi-structured interviews, where each child was listened to individually by a member of the research team. Wherever possible, the same researcher was assigned to the same child for each of the three sessions. The remaining 15 minutes of each session consisted of a group discussion. In addition, the children were asked to complete a weekend activity diary and, in the Midlands primary school, children also wrote essays about their favourite and desired possessions.

In the secondary schools, the semi-structured interviews were replaced by questionnaires which were completed by all children present in the class on that day. Twelve children were then selected from each school year at random but within gender groups to participate in two group discussion sessions. In the event, it was not possible to meet the full quota for the male group discussions in the Midlands school because of high levels of absenteeism.

The research covered a wide range of issues. The questionnaires embraced family background, friends and where they lived (in the junior schools only), possessions, activities, economic socialisation, self-esteem and perceptions of their socio-economic status. The group discussions included advertising, techniques used to persuade parents to buy particular goods, the exchange of goods between friends, clothing, birthdays and, for older children only, sexual activity and drug use.

Questionnaires were subjected to both quantitative and qualitative analysis. Quantitative analysis was carried out using the Statistical Package for the Social Sciences (SPSS). The majority of the analysis consisted of cross tabulations of dependent variables by socio-economic status and, in some instances, age and sex; chi-square statistical tests were carried out where appropriate. Continuous dependent variables were analysed using t-tests.

All group discussions were taped and subsequently transcribed, along with all responses to open-ended questions in the questionnaires. Qualitative analysis was carried out using the same techniques as described for the analysis of the parents' group discussions. Again, we have attempted to allow the children to speak for themselves wherever possible, although their names have been changed. Verbatim quotations are followed by: an indication of the catchment area of the school – MA = more affluent, LA = less affluent; the sex of the child speaking wherever possible – M = male, F = female, GU = gender unknown; and the age group of the child. (In a small number of the taped group discussions in which both boys and girls took part it proved impossible to identify the sex of the child.)

Throughout the book, extensive use is made of verbatim quotation from the discussions. This gives a more vivid impression of the way in which parents and children think, talk and behave. However, it is included purely for illustrative purposes and should be read in the context of the surrounding commentary. Some important points are not easy to illustrate in this way, and the presence or absence of a verbatim quotation is not necessarily an indication of the importance of a particular topic.

BIBLIOGRAPHY

Adler, R P et al, *The Effects of Television Advertising on Children*, New York: Lexington Books, 1980.

Banks, J and Johnson, P, *Children and Household Living Standards*, London: Institute for Fiscal Studies, 1993.

Bradshaw, J and Stimson, C, *Use and Contribution of Child Benefit within the Family Budget*, York: Department of Social Policy and Social Work, University of York (forthcoming).

Bradshaw, J, *Household Budgets and Living Standards*, York: Joseph Rowntree Foundation, 1993.

Bradshaw, J (ed), *Budget Standards for the United Kingdom*, Aldershot: Avebury Press, 1993.

Bradshaw, J and Holmes, H, *Living on the Edge*, Newcastle: Child Poverty Action Group, 1989.

Burgess, R, *The Ethics of Educational Research*, London: Falmer, 1989.

Burgess, R (ed), *Field Methods in the Study of Education*, London: Falmer, 1985.

Central Statistical Office, *Social Focus on Children*, London: HMSO, 1994.

Central Statistical Office, *General Household Survey*, London: HMSO, 1992.

Children's Rights Development Unit, *UK Agenda Report 4: An adequate standard of living*, London: Children's Rights Development Unit, 1994.

Cohen, R, Coxall, J, Craig, G and Sadiq-Sangster, A, *Hardship Britain: being poor in the 1990s*, London: Child Poverty Action Group, 1992.

Coleman, J C and Hendry, L, *The Nature of Adolescence*, London: Routledge, 1990 (second edition).

Comstock, G, *Television and the American Child*, California: Academic Press Inc, 1991.

Department of Social Security, *Households Below Average Income: a statistical analysis 1979 – 1991/92*, London: HMSO, 1994.

Dickens, R, Fry, V and Pashardes, P, *The Cost of Children and the Welfare State*, York: Joseph Rowntree Foundation, 1994.

Ditch, J, Pickles, S and Whiteford, P, *The New Structure of Child Benefit: a review*, London: Coalition for Child Benefit, 1992.

Dittmar, Helga, *The Social Psychology of Material Possessions*, Hemel Hempstead: Harvester Wheatsheaf, 1992.

Dobson, B, Beardsworth, A, Keil, T and Walker, R, *Diet, Choice and Poverty*, London: Family Policy Studies Centre, 1994.

Eckstein, J (ed), *Cultural Trends*, Vol 17, London: Policy Studies Institute, 1993.

Field, F, *What Price a Child? a historical review of the relative cost of dependants*, Studies of the Social Security System No. 8, London: Policy Studies Institute, 1985.

Fowles, J, *Why Viewers Watch: a reappraisal of television's effect*, London: Sage, 1992.

Furby, L, 'Possession in humans: an exploratory study of its meaning and motivation', *Social Behaviour and Personality*, 6 (1), 1978.

Furnham, A, 'Children's understanding of the economic world', *Australian Journal of Education*, 30: 3, 1986.

Glendinning, C and Millar, J (eds), *Women and Poverty in Britain: the 1990s*, London: Harvester Wheatsheaf, 1992.

Goldberg, M, 'A quasi-experiment assessing the effectiveness of TV advertising directed at children', *Journal of Marketing Research*, 27, 1990.

Goldstein, J H, *Television Advertising and Children: a review of the research*, Brussels: prepared for Toy Manufacturers of Europe, 1992.

Gunter, B and McAleer, J L, *Children and Television: the one eyed monster?* London: Routledge, 1990.

Hagenaars, A and de Vos, K, 'The definition and measurement of poverty', *Journal of Human Resources*, 22, 1988.

Hedges, A and Hyatt, J, *Attitudes of Beneficiaries to Child Benefit and Benefits for Young People*, London: Social and Community Planning Research, 1985.

Hill, M, 'Children and poverty', *Benefits*, 3, 1992.

Isler, L, Popper, E and Ward S, 'Children's purchase requests and parental responses', *Journal of Advertising Research*, 27, 1987.

Jahoda, G, 'The construction of economic reality by some Glaswegian children', *European Journal of Social Psychology*, Vol. 9, 1979.

Jenkins, S, *Winners and Losers: a portrait of the UK income distribution during the 1980s*, University of Wales, Swansea: Department of Economics Discussion Paper Series No. 94-07, 1994.

Kempson, E, Bryson, A and Rawlingson, K, *Hard Times: how poor families make ends meet*, London: Policy Studies Unit, 1994.

Kumar, V, *Poverty and Inequality in the UK: the effects on children*, London: National Children's Bureau, 1993.

Lareau, A, *Home Advantage: social class and parental intervention in elementary education*, London: Falmer, 1989.

Leccese, D, 'Toy advertising and TV', *Playthings*, 1989.

Liebert, R M and Sprafkin, E, *The Early Window: effects of television on children and youth*, Oxford: Pergamon Press, 1988.

Mack, J and Lansley, S, *Poor Britain*, London: George Allen and Unwin, 1985.

McNeal, J U, *Kids as Customers: a handbook of marketing to children*, New York: Lexington Books, 1992.

Mitchell, D and Cooke, K, 'Costs of childrearing', in R Walker and E Parker (eds), *Money Matters*, London: Sage, 1988.

Oldfield, N, and Yu, A S, *The Cost of a Child: living standards for the 1990s*, London: Child Poverty Action Group, 1993.

Oppenheim, C, *The Cost of a Child*, London: Child Poverty Action Group, 1990.

Piachaud, D, *Children and Poverty*, London: Child Poverty Action Group, 1981.

Piachaud, D, *The Cost of a Child*, London: Child Poverty Action Group, 1979.

Reicken, G and Yavas, U, 'Children's general, product and brand specific attitudes to television commercials', *International Journal of Advertising*, 9, 1990.

Roll, J, *Babies and Money: birth trends and costs*, London: Family Policy Studies Centre, 1986.

Silverstone, R and Hirsch, E (eds), *Consuming Technologies – media and information in domestic space*, London: Routledge, 1992.

Walker, R, Middleton, S and Thomas, M, *Mostly on the Children: the significance of child benefit in family budgets*, Loughborough: Centre for Research in Social Policy, CRSP Working Paper 218, 1993.

Walker, R, 'Consensual approaches to poverty lines and social security', *Journal of Social Policy*, 16, 1987.

Walsh, A and Lister, R, *Mother's Lifeline*, London: Child Poverty Action Group, 1985.

Ward, S and Wackman, D, 'Children's purchase influence attempts and parent yielding'. *Journal of Marketing Research*, 9, 1972.

Young, B, *Television Advertising and Children*, Oxford: Clarendon Press, 1990.

The Cost of a Child

Living standards for the 1990s

Nina Oldfield and Autumn C S Yu

This new study adds to the growing evidence that income support does not meet even the most minimal needs of children. The research was carried out by the Family Budget Unit at the University of York, and is the first systematic reassessment of the basic benefit scales since the Beveridge Report in 1948.

The study uses two 'budget standards', or specific baskets of goods and services which when priced represent two standards of living. There is a modest-but-adequate standard representing the cost of the average child, and a low-cost budget reduced to necessities.

Behind the bare statistics lie important findings which make a crucial contribution to tackling current issues – including VAT on fuel, the position of lone parents, subsidised childcare, child benefit and levels of income support.

88 pages   0 946744 56 4   October 1993   £6.95

Please send .... copy/ies of *The Cost of a Child* @ £6.95 each (incl p&p).

I enclose a cheque/PO for £ .... payable to CPAG Ltd

Name ....

Address ....

....

.... Postcode ....

Return payment with order to CPAG Ltd, 1-5 Bath Street, London EC1V 9PY

Poverty: the Facts

Carey Oppenheim

**"Poverty takes away the tools to create the building blocks for the future –
your 'life chances'. It steals away the opportunity to have a life unmarked by
sickness, a decent education, a secure home and a long retirement. It stops
people being able to plan ahead. It stops people being able to take control
of their lives."**

Using new figures released since the last edition (1990), *Poverty: the Facts*
reveals all you need to know about the growth of poverty in recent years,
changing patterns of regional inequality, the increased vulnerability of children to
poverty, and comparisons with other EC countries. There is coverage of recent
debates on poverty and its definition, as well as of questions like universal
benefits vs means-testing, and 'is there an underclass?'.

With its informed coverage of issues such as race, homelessness, health, and the
sexual politics of deprivation, *Poverty: the Facts* is without doubt the most
comprehensive and authoritative assessment of poverty in the UK.

216 pages   0 946744 49 1   1993   £6.95

**Send a cheque/PO for £6.95 (incl. p&p) to
CPAG Ltd, 1-5 Bath Street, London EC1V 9PY**